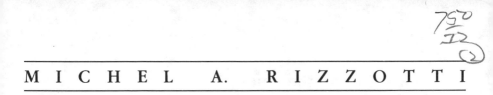

MICHEL A. RIZZOTTI

D0618749

GOD, MYTH, AND METAPHOR

THE PROFANE REALITY OF THE GODDESS

Northshore Publishing, Los Angeles

GOD, MYTH, AND METAPHOR
The Profane Reality of the Goddess

Published by:

Northshore Publishing
P.O. Box 25398
Los Angeles, CA 90025

Copyright ©1992 by Michel A. Rizzotti
Printed in the United States of America

Library of Congress Catalog Card Number: 91-091489

Publisher's Cataloguing in Publication
(Prepared by Quality Books Inc.)

Rizzotti, Michel A.
  God, Myth, and Metaphor: the profane reality of the Goddess/
Michel A. Rizzotti.

  p. cm.
  Includes bibliographical references and index.
  ISBN 0-9630980-3-9

  1. Religion—Research—Methodology. 2. Mythology. I. Title.

BL41.R5 1992   230.04
                                 QB191-1822

To *Michelle*

Contents

The Language of Myth

*They say it's a wise child that knows its father,
but it's a damn sight wiser child that knows its
own mother.*

Robertson Davies,
"What's Bred in the Bone"

When Gustave Flaubert said, *Madame Bovary, c'est moi!* he meant to say something about himself as well as something about the novel. Notably, that the narrative reveals the world of its creator.

Genesis and Exodus were written by priests. These priests were also scribes who also acted as legal functionaries of their time. Hardly any king, nor kingdom, could do without their services. The written accounts of Genesis and Exodus are a literary "creation" that generated the "world" of the Bible as we know it. What these anonymous writers do not reveal, however, is the purpose and motive for which they wrote these narratives.

The creation narrative of Genesis reveals a God overly concerned with pro**creation** and the genealogy of his people. On the other hand Exodus describes Yahweh as the prototype of the patriarchal herdsman: a God opposed to other gods. And as we will see he is especially opposed to the fertility cults of the Goddess. A close analysis of these narratives also reveals that the "monotheistic" and jealous God of the Bible has forged his sacred identity because of his **opposition** to the **profane** reality of the Goddess.

Long before Yahweh made his appearance, the social systems of Old Europe were, in all likelihood, predominantly matriarchal. Archaeological evidence shows that many attributes associated with the Great Goddess played a substantial role in the development of early forms of mythical expressions and cultic life.

There is enough evidence to suggest that these peaceful and egalitarian cultures of Old Europe were slowly decimated by the invasion of Indo-European pastoral tribes. These horse riding warriors, along with their thundering gods, began to impose the supremacy of their patriarchal ways. The Goddess was slowly subdued by force and her precepts began to lose ground.

As evidenced in the Bible she was eventually supplanted by a jealous God who demanded exclusive worship. One prominent aspect of the patriarchal identity of the God of the Old Testament finds its origin in the **exclusion** of the other gods and goddesses from its religious realm.

Genesis and Exodus relate that Yahweh, the people, and the law are so closely intertwined together that the religion of Israel is perhaps better defined as monolithic rather than monotheistic. Moreover, these narratives reveal that the power of the **sacred** is closely connected to Yahweh as the "Holy One". His **word** revealed in the ten commandments is consolidated in the sacred power of the law. Yet the written law is the exclusive dominion of the priests who interpret and guard it. These priests made sure when they wrote the Bible that they would have exclusive dominion over the mystery of the sacred. They also made sure that no other divinity would come and challenge the foundation of their authority.

In the movie the Wizard of Oz there is a relevant example of *deus ex machina;* ie, the props used in the theater to portray God's supernatural powers. The film shows how the Wizard uses all kinds of contraptions to foster his power and inspire fear. Yet as soon as Dorothy unveils him pulling the levers behind the curtains, the real source of his power is revealed. Stripped of his secrets, he becomes powerless. Only then can Dorothy assume her new-found assertiveness.

I cannot think of a more appropriate analogy to relate how the power of the sacred is generated by the cultic apparatus; how this power is perpetuated by taboos which are promoted by tradition and implemented by the patriarchal hierarchy of the priestly office.

The exclusion of the Goddess from the Old Testament narratives illustrates one important aspect of the **profane** reality. Yet another of its expressions is related in the Book of Job.

The narrative describes the painful experience of a character called Job who is a victim of God's unpredictable whim. At the outset, the hero is described as rich and famous, a model of loyalty, and God's favorite servant. Suddenly, he is punished for no apparent reason. As a consequence, he loses all his possessions and his body is afflicted with horrible diseases. As all of these curses befall him he is

excluded from the whole community. All the while the hero insists on his innocence and questions the reason for his unfortunate fate.

The end is as unpredictable as the beginning. God finally restores his servant with greater glory than he had at the outset. But something important happened to Job during his dreadful ordeal. In the denouement he acknowledges that he "sees" God, whereas before he had only "heard" of him.

What happened to our hero to allow such a vision?

•

As described in the Bible, the **sacred**—or the holy—has been throughout the centuries the central theme of most religious beliefs and ritual practices. The holy is perhaps the matrix of religion as we know it. Yet the profane, which plays a significant role in the development of the sacred, has been deliberately discounted. To illustrate how important the dichotomy between the sacred and the profane is, just think of the primordial opposition between:

God	vs	Satan
good	vs	evil
sacred	vs	profane

As we will see in the following chapters, the reality of the **profane** is as vital as the sacred. Yet it's only one aspect of the three principles that make up the **whole** religious reality. The two others are the **sacred** and the **wholly other.** Together they form a single **dynamic** entity.

In the second part of the book we will parallel the latter sacred triad to the Holy Trinity. Namely, God the Father, God the Son, and the Holy Spirit. Again one notices the conspicuous absence of the Goddess principle from the divine triune reality. The reason is simple. The nature of the profane is described as an **excluded** and **hidden** reality, hence not readily apparent. Since the sacred is the center of religion, the profane has been its overshadowed and segregated reality—herein lies the Goddess. And to complement these two principles the wholly other is the transcendental sphere where both realities meet. In essence, the religious experience could be described in terms of the dynamic interrelation between these three principles: the sacred, the profane, and the wholly other.

•

Myth, as a form of language, is the **medium** *par excellence* thru which the sacred is revealed. The language of myth **separates** the words and actions of the gods from the ordinary world. Myth creates a different setting and separates the boundaries between:

the divine	vs	the human
the **extra**ordinary	vs	the ordinary
the celestial	vs	the terrestrial
the **super**natural	vs	the natural

Mythical stories describe the coming into being of a **new** reality through the actions of the gods and super-heroes. They relate the origin of an effective reality as a prototype for human thought or action.

Myth discloses the primordial. It introduces how a new mythical reality came into being for the first time. The time of myth is a time before time. Mircea Eliade calls it *in illo tempore.* The space of myth is the space beyond the ordinary world. The protagonists in myth belong to an exclusive and other-wordly sphere restricted to the gods and super-heroes. In their **super**natural world they are **separated** from the ordinariness of the human condition.

In other words, myth describes and legitimizes the **powers** that generate and rule the "world" and the beings that live in it.

Originally, the Greek word for "mythos" meant word, language, or message. It was differentiated from "logos" which also meant word or speech but implied discussion or argument. As the Greek definition suggests, the language of myth is authoritative, it is not open to argument. As such, myth inaugurates and imprints a new reality.

But more specifically, myth expounds a **mentality;** ie, the mode of thought, the mores, and the ethics peculiar to an individual or a collectivity. The Bible, for instance, is the unique compendium of the people of Israel. In the creation myth of Genesis a new "world" is conceived literally. The style and language of the narrative reflect the peculiar customs, the culture, and the religion of its people. By knowing its writers we can more fully understand the society in which the "world" of the Bible was created.

Unfortunately today too much emphasis is put on the myth's significance as an invented story, as being false and untrue. It's a deplorable misuse since behind its exotic and sometimes obscure language, myth, particularly from other cultures and ancient times, reveals the synopsis of a whole cultural reality, namely, a mentality. And though it is easy to translate the words of myth from a foreign language, it is quite difficult to convey the whole original significance as it was understood by the people who literally lived by its meaningful message. *Traduttore traditore;* ie, the translator betrayor formula here is appropriate.

Similarly, mythical super-heroes like Superman, Wonder Woman, Batman, or Mickey Mouse, reveal an important aspect of the American culture. These **super**natural heroes represent a singular aspect of American cultural identity. They also reveal a unique facet of the collective *psyche*.

Consequently, myth as a medium plays a greater role in the development of a culture than it is given credit for. Think of how the myth of Oedipus inspired Sigmund Freud's psychological theory. Or, how myth played a vital role in the creation and propagation of world religions. And, how the creation myths of Genesis are at the origin of the Judeo-Christian "world" as we know it.

As we will see in the third part of the book, myth also effects society and culture in a dramatic way. Particularly in terms of the cosmological, historical, and ideological roles it plays in the integration of society and in the development of a national identity.

The native Zuni Pueblo of New Mexico is a perfect example of how myth creates and regulates a **cosmos:** namely, a meaningful "world" unique to its people. It is also a perfect example of a profane reality that survived amid an overpowering American dream.

Myth has been quintessential in the historic development of nationalism in the province of Quebec, Canada, where it has been ultimately expressed in terms of a quest for "Independence".

Myth also played an active role in the ideological edification of the American identity. In the nineteenth century for instance, the "image" of George Washington was faithfully eulogized—better still mythologized—in a widespread national campaign. The main purpose of this crusade was to **create** a national identity and to generate a political consensus in order to consolidate the political power in Washington D.C.

This mythologizing process also promoted and maintained the development of what Riane Eisler calls an "androcratic"—patriarchal—order in the New World.[1] This is partly the result of the exclusion of the profane reality of the Goddess from the Bible.

•

We have already stated that myth is a unique form of **language.** Consequently, linguistics, but more specifically, semantics, are helpful to elaborate on a mythical process that enables us to identify myth whenever present in the **story,** but more particularly in the narrative. In the arrangement outlined below myth is expressed in terms of a "thematic" sequence:[2]

---

[1] Riane Eisler, The Chalice & the Blade, San Francisco, Harper & Row, 1987.

[2] The original idea and sequence is taken from A.J. Greimas, Structural Semantics: an Attempt at a Method, Lincoln, University of Nebraska Press, 1983, 180-183. I have introduced my own sequence which may neither be endorsed nor approved by the author.

the setting
the hero
the quest
the obstacle
the mentor
the outcome

When the sequence is applied to a myth like the creation narrative of Genesis the model looks like this:

the setting .... the **beginning** of the "world"
the hero .... God
the quest .... order and meaning
the obstacle .... void, darkness, and chaos
the mentor .... speech and language
the outcome .... the **Genesis** of the Bible

The fundamental object, or purpose, of the sequence is entirely centered on **communication,** which is at the core of all mythical function.

•

Right "in the beginning" of Genesis God uses his speech to **communicate** his "world" to us. Language, to say the least, is a primordial tool.

Then God **said,** "Let us make man in our image,
after our likeness. . .[3]

This is also true in respect to the metaphor. The next example illustrates precisely what we mean. Jesus says:

I am the door[4]

The quote above is vivid enough. It reveals how much emphasis is put on the significance of the **word** and the **metaphor.**[5]

---

[3] Gen. 1:26

[4] John 10:9

[5] It would be ludicrous to think that Jesus' words are meant to convey that he is a swinging piece of wood that separates two spaces. Even the most fundamental believers, those who believe in the literal meaning of the Bible, admit it is a metaphor. But why do these same people have such great difficulty in recognizing that the whole Bible is written in the same fashion, or should we say, in the same "Spirit"! Is not the parable, which is nothing other than an extended metaphor, the key to the whole Scriptures?

The implied meaning of the metaphor is that Jesus is the **"Way"** from one state being to another. His "Word" holds the key to an-**other** "world" of meaning. Hence only those who understand the true essence of the Word are able to gain access to his spiritual message.

the literal   vs   the metaphorical
the material   vs   the spiritual
the physical   vs   the metaphysical

At the outset, the literal sense of the word is confined by the rigid and material aspect of reality; ie, the door, which could even imply a barrier. The true essence of the Word is to transcend the physical, the material, and the literal into the spiritual realm of language: the metaphorical.[6]

---

[6] The metaphorical implies much more than meets the eye. Its chief function lies in the **Spirit** of the "Word" rather than the letter of the word. Hence, the metaphor is a shift in meaning and an expansion of being. See Paul Ricoeur, The Rule of Metaphor, University of Toronto Press, Toronto, 1975.

PART ONE

OLD TESTAMENT TRADITION: One God, One People

*The cherub with his flaming sword is hereby
commanded to leave his guard at the tree of life,
and when he does, the whole creation will be
consumed, and appear infinite, and holy,
whereas it now appears finite and corrupt.*

William Blake,
"The Marriage of Heaven and Hell"

GENESIS: The Hidden Goddess of the Creation Myth

The creation myth of Genesis is typical of many creation myths that describe the beginning of a **new** cultural, religious, and cosmological reality. It is similar to Egyptian, Akkadian, Babylonian, and Iranian cosmogonies.[1] These accounts show how God uses his **word** to articulate a new mythical "world". The word, and consequently **language,** is the medium that allows the divinity to communicate to "man" his creation.

the setting	. . . .	the **beginning** of the "world"
the hero	. . . .	God
the quest	. . . .	order and meaning
the obstacle	. . . .	void, darkness, and chaos
the mentor	. . . .	speech and language
the outcome	. . . .	the **Genesis** of the Bible

The first book of the Bible is appropriately called Genesis, which is the Greek translation of the Hebrew "in the beginning". As such, it is the introductory **setting** for the story of the people of Israel as recounted in the first five books of the Bible: namely, Genesis, Exodus, Leviticus, Numbers, and Deuteronomy. These books are also called the Pentateuch and the Torah.

---

[1] Hermann Gunkel, The Legends of Genesis, Chicago, Open Court, 1901.

God did not physically write these words. Several unknown priests did. Extensive biblical studies show that several versions of similar stories were compiled together by a redactor called "R" into one single narrative. His final compilation shows how important his role has been in creating the Bible. He was responsible for putting together into one narrative several versions of often contradictory accounts that, until recently, were believed to have been written by Moses.[2]

Genesis 1 thru 3, which is the subject of this chapter, is divided according to three sources of composition:

> verses 1:1 to 2:3 are accredited to P
> verse 2:4a is attributed to R
> verses 2:4b to 3:24 are written by J

P refers to the priestly source, who is also the largest contributor to the Pentateuch. He has been given this designation because his accounts are mainly concerned in securing priestly interests. The second source, which is a single phrase, is written by R, the Redactor. This single verse links the two sources into one uniform account of the creation. J, the writer of the second version of the creation of "man", as well as the fall, is called the Yahwist because in his accounts he refers to God as Yahweh.

P

Gen. 1:1 In the beginning God created the heavens and the earth. The earth was without form and void, and darkness was upon the face of the deep; and the Spirit of God was moving over the face of the waters.
And God **said,** "Let there be light"; and there was light. And God saw that the light was good; and God **separated** the light from darkness. God **called** the light Day, and the darkness he called Night. And there was evening and there was morning, one day.

The first paragraph above is more of an introduction to God's creative activity which really begins with:[3]

---

[2] See Richard Elliott Friedman, Who Wrote the Bible?, New York, Summit Books, 1987.

[3] The first verse can also be rendered "in the beginning of" which also allows the translation: "When God began to create the heavens and earth". The Torah, The Jewish Publication Society of America, Philadelphia, 1962.

God literally uses his **speech** to create the world. **Language** is God's primordial tool. Without it he could not reveal his existence, neither could he describe his creation.

If we make a parallel with this to the first verses of the Gospel of John we find that the Evangelist also identifies Christ with the ''Word'' in the beginning. The example is in itself an important clue to the nature of the ''Word'' in God's creative endeavor.[4]

Jn. 1:1 In the beginning was the **Word,** and the **Word** was with God, and the **Word** was God. He was in the beginning with God; all things were made through him, and without him was not anything made that was made.

Similar ancient Babylonian, Egyptian, and Indian cosmogonies also imply a divine power inherent in the word itself which when uttered brings out **order.** Numerous ancient myths provide a good example of the likeness of the creative power of the divine word. In ancient Egypt the god Ptah of Memphis, in a comparable fashion, created the world through his spoken word.[5] While Sumerian myths describe how divinities first plan their creation by thinking, and then the world comes into being through the power of speech.

Based on the content of the biblical text above, it appears that speech is one of God's primordial activities.[6] Language allows the divinity to reveal his creation to us. We might say that the existence of language precedes the existence of God, since before the first words of Genesis are spoken there is nothingness, and before the order of syntax is put forth there is chaos. The Bible—from the Latin *ta biblia* which means the little books—is sacred precisely because the words have been recorded, but mostly because they have been preserved for posterity by the Priests.

---

[4] Yet orthodox interpretation of the significance of the ''word'' is commonly understood as being an expression of God's will. See Gerhard von Rad, on the Word of God in ''Old Testament Theology'', London, Oliver and Boyd Ltd, 1966.

[5] Siegfried Morenz, Egyptian Religion, New York, Cornell University Press, 1973, 159 f. Another interesting aspect about ancient Egyptian creation myths is God Khnum's creative ability as craftsman and procreator compared to the biblical God who molded man from the ground and created woman from man.

[6] The noted Old Testament scholar Gerhard von Rad explains: ''This naming is thus both an act of copying and an act of appropriative ordering, by which man intellectually objectifies the creatures for himself. Thus one may say that something is said here about the origin of language, so long as one does not emphasize the discovery of external words but rather that inner appropriation of recognizing and interpreting, which happens in language.'' in, Genesis, London, SCM Press, 1963, 81.

Hence, God's rhetoric describes the "beginning" of a reality which is the Bible itself. As such, the Bible is foremost a literary **creation,** albeit a sacred one for the believers.[7]

The narrative does not explain to whom God speaks, nor from where. God here is an *individuum vaguum;* ie, a vague and imageless individual. He nevertheless uses speech, which is a human characteristic. He does so without using the configuration of an *individuum certum,* in other words, without assuming the identity —or the image—of a person. Consequently, the creative powers of the **word** supersedes any other human attribute.

Furthermore, the way the narrative reports God's words is analogous to the way lords or sovereigns dictated their will to the scribes. As the account reveals, the LORD speaks and his will is being transcribed. In this context, the account links the ancient oral tradition to the written.[8]

Moreover, the biblical Hebrew alphabet is made up primarily of 22 consonants. In the unvocalized Hebrew alphabet, speech is necessary to give **meaning** to the unvocalized words, otherwise the letters are a meaningless and chaotic code. Only with the spoken word are the vowels uttered. By exhaling one's **breath** into the letters, the alphabet miraculously takes on a **life** and **Spirit** of its own, and words finally become meaningful.

As the text shows, God speaks from nowhere and to nobody in particular. Yet he becomes preoccupied with the order and plan of things to which he is about to give names. He also becomes involved in the **separation** of the world into a set order of categories; most obvious of which is the division of time into seven days and the classification of his creation by **name.**[9]

The name giving activity in creation is not exclusive to the Bible either. It is also prevalent in the ancient Near Eastern mythology where it was seen as an exercise of sovereignty, especially in terms of property and dominion.[10]

The act of **separating** and **naming** reveals another important facet of the divine creative activity. This classification of words and names can be appropriately referred to as a biblical glossary.[11] This

---

[7] Northrop Frye, The Great Code, Toronto, Academic Press Canada, 1982, XVI.

[8] And as we have already mentioned writing and recording were the monopoly of the scribes.

[9] Paul Ricoeur has suggested that there is something to be said about the "metaphorical" as being at the origin of logical thought; Paul Ricoeur, The rule of Metaphor, Toronto, University of Toronto Press, 1977.

[10] As Gerhard von Rad puts it; "let us remind ourselves once more that name-giving in the ancient Orient was primarily an exercise of sovereignty, of command." in Genesis, Ibid., 81.

[11] Emile Durkheim and Marcel Mauss, Primitive Classification, Chicago, University of Chicago Press, 1963.

order becomes in effect a description of God's identifiable creation; ie, the **inventory** of the property to which "man" can "have dominion". The definition of things and beings is setting the stage for the "world" of the Bible.

Numerous studies made on "primitive" classification reveal how this complex display of symbolic representations and relationships is meant to represent the grounds of social organization. A typical example is the system of moieties in tribes of Australia. It is also prevalent in the astronomical, astrological, geomantic, and horoscopic divinatory systems of ancient China, of which Taoism is a fine example. Closer to home, the Zuni Pueblo of New Mexico is yet another fine example of how classification is at the core of its mythology and cosmology. We will further develop the classification aspect of mythology later in the chapter on Zuni.[12]

In the 6th day, his last day of activity, God ultimately utters the concept of his most important creation.

> Gen. 1:26 Then God **said,** "Let **us** make man in **our image,** after our **likeness** . . ." So God created man in his own **image,** in the **image** of God he created him; male and female he created them.

God speaks in the first person until verse 26, but as he gets closer to the pinnacle of his creation he finally opts for the plural form. The change is fundamental, especially in view of its underlining message.

The first and obvious sense of "Let us" could be taken as "abstract plural" or "plural of intensity". In Hebrew, for instance, the word for man—*'adam*—also has a collective meaning and may be used here in the sense of "mankind".

There may be yet another connotation implied by the plurality. Before the people of Israel adopted Yahweh as their only God, they worshipped El, which was also the God of the neighboring Canaanites.

El, which means literally *the* God, shared his title with his wife, goddess Asherah. Both had the epithets of the "creator" and the "creatress". Archaeological findings at Quntillet ᶜAjrud show that not only El, but also Yahweh was associated with a divine wife named Asherah.[13]

[12] Emile Durkheim, Ibid.

[13] See article by David Noel Freedman, Yahweh of Samaria and his Asherah, in, *Biblical Archeologist,* December 1987, 241-249.

19

J

Gen. 2:7 then the LORD God **formed** man of the dust from the ground, and **breathed** into his nostrils the **breath of life; and man became a living being. And the LORD God **planted** a **garden** in Eden, in the east; and there he put the man whom he had formed. And out of the ground the LORD God made to grow every tree that is pleasant to the sight and good for food, the tree of life also in the **midst** of the garden, and the tree of the knowledge of good and evil.

In Hebrew, the words **genesis, beginning,** and **birth** are all synonyms. So are the words **Spirit, wind, breath,** and **life.** They all point to **pro-creation** as the **genesis** of life itself.

In the narrative God proceeds to mold from the soil *'adam*—man—which is taken from *'adamah*—the ground—and like a potter he molds his creation. Adam finally "becomes a living being" when God breathes into it the **"breath of life".**

Although in the first account "man", the only creation that is able to understand God's words, is created on the last day, all that was created prior to him was created specifically for him. In chapter two, however, "man" is the **center** of attention, everything evolves around him.

In chapter one, the creation is "spoken" out of chaos and nothingness into an orderly syntax. Whereas in the second version God creates man to put him in the **center** of a **tree garden** called Eden. Man is purposefully created by God as a "tiller" and "keeper" of his garden. At the outset, the relationship between God and man is established as one of land-LORD and keeper. J marks a clear distinction between the sovereignty of God over his garden and man; ie, the separation between the creator and **his** creation, between the master and **his** slave.

Unlike in the former version, God enables man to "call" and "name" every living creature; an important role he had kept for himself before. In doing so he allows man to share his divine power of speech and appropriation.

Gardens, particularly fertile fields, were the marked possession of great Kings. And as we see in verses 2:4b-6 the writer uses words like "plant", "field", "earth", "herb", "sprung up", "rain", "till the ground", and "soil" from which "man" was made. All these terms have an agricultural connotation and expose the fertility symbolism of the passage.

Finally, in the **midst** of this garden God **planted** the tree of

life and the tree of knowledge of good and evil. And God commanded "man" not to eat from the tree of knowledge of good and evil
or else he will die. The theme of the **center,** as we will see throughout this book, is primordial.[14] Here, the narrative describes both
trees of life and of good and evil as being in the **middle** of the
garden.[15]

Popular misconception still associates the forbidden fruit with
the apple. There is no mention of an apple tree in the text. The con-
fusion probably stemmed from the similarity between the Latin
words *malum,* evil, and *malus,* apple. The two terms were apparently confused in the course of history.

Concerned about man's solitude God decides to give him a
"helper". The narrative goes on to describe a shift in the normal
role of pro**creation.** Ironically, God and man appropriate the function of begetting: God takes the "woman" out of the "man". Then
the "man" called his companion "Woman" because she was "taken
out" of him. This inversion reveals a fundamental aspect of ancient
Judaism. It lies in the patriarchal appropriation of woman's fecundity and the strict opposition to the fertility cults associated with
the Goddess. Any implicit allusion to the Goddess worship, especially as typified here by Asherah, has been obliterated from the
narrative. The first commandment given by Yahweh is clear: he
opposes any other divinity including that of the Goddess.[16]

Deut. 16:21 You shall not plant any **tree as an Ashe'rah** beside
the altar of the LORD your God which you shall make.
And you shall not set up a pillar, which the LORD your
God hates.

The first Commandment is explicit and categorical, any worship
of or reference to any other god is prohibited. The *ethos* implement-

---

[14] Mircea Eliade, Cosmos and History, New York, Harper And Row, 1959, 12 ff.

[15] The word midst could be translated as the center or middle. The Torah uses the word
"bad" instead of evil, which gives a more pragmatic significance, see The Torah, Ibid.

[16] Asherah was also known as Athirat, which is a dialectical variant. She is also referred to
in the Bible as Ashtoreth, Ashteroth, Astoreth, Astaroth, Ashterathite, Anath, Beeshterah,
Elath, and Baalath. The title "holy one", is also believed to be one of her epithets. See
Merlin Stone, When God Was a Woman, San Diego, A Harvest Book/HBJ Book, 1976,
163-170.

ed by the priests through the ages reinforced this belief. The narrative of Genesis implicitly **overshadows** the fact that the tree is a metaphor for the Goddess and a symbol of **Asherah.**

The fundamental point to be made about biblical patriarchy is related to the genealogy of the people as a **tribal clan.** Only with strict ethical laws and prohibitions could men control women's fertility and their progeny. In addition, these laws legally reinforced the fact that women were a closely supervised "property" of men who became their controlling agents of fecundity.[17]

Gen. 2:24 Therefore a man leaves his father and his mother and cleaves to his wife, and they become one flesh.

The above verse of Genesis, which is a reference to matriarchy, is in plain contradiction with the patriarchal customs of Judaism. According to ancient Jewish customs, it is not the man who leaves his parents but the woman.[18] This passage may suggest remnants of a matriarchal past. Such a contradiction in context to the rest of the narrative is only one among the many clues that show the full extent of the exclusion and opposition to the fertility cults of the Goddess in the Bible.

•

Gen. 3:1 Now the serpent was more **subtle** than any other wild creature that the LORD God had made. He said to the woman, "Did God say, 'You shall not eat of any tree of the garden'?" And the woman said to the serpent, "We may eat of the fruit of the trees of the garden; but God said, 'You shall not eat of the fruit of the tree which is in the **midst of the garden,** neither shall you touch it, lest you **die**' ". But the serpent said to the woman, "You will not die. For God knows that when you eat of it your **eyes will be opened,** and you will be like God, knowing good and evil."

the setting . . . . the tree garden of Eden

---

[17] Denise L. Carmody, Judaism, in, Women and World Religions, ed. by Arvind Sharma, Albany, State University of New York Press, 1987. I cannot help thinking, whenever I come across similar examples, of how men are fascinated and also envious of women's fertility. It seems that men had to compensate for their sense of inadequacy in this regard by a propensity to dominate religion and mythology, since they are unable to control nature. The powerful God depicted as the male creator figure is just one example.

[18] "Curiously, the statement about forsaking father and mother does not quite correspond to the patriarchal family customs of Ancient Israel, for after the marriage the wife breaks loose from her family much more than the man does from his. Does this tendentious statement perhaps preserve something from a time of matriarchal culture?" Gerhard von Rad, Genesis, a Commentary, London, SCM Press, 1963, 83.

the quest	. . . .	knowledge of good and evil
the hero	. . . .	the woman
the obstacle	. . . .	God's ban
the mentor	. . . .	the serpent
the outcome	. . . .	Eve: the mother of all living

In The Fall, the events that describe the beginning of the relationship between the protagonists are doomed at the outset. The narrative depicts the characters entangled in a situation in which the quest for knowledge and the emulation of God are greater than the fear of punishment. The crux of the narrative reveals that the desire to be **like** God prevails.[19] But because of their deliberate disobedience, Adam and Eve are thrown out of the garden. As a consequence, they will be excluded from God's presence and property. The narrative makes it explicitly clear that the woman is to be held responsible for man's alienation from his God.

As we have suggested earlier, the garden of Eden is full of fertility symbols. The four rivers that flow in the garden allude to it. The trees bearing the most alluring of fruits denote it. And the presence of the serpent confirms it.

The serpent, a Canaanite symbol of life, health, and fecundity, simply strengthens the fertility theme of the whole narrative. Not to mention that the **"tree** of **life"** is obviously another prominent metaphor for fertility.[20] But the most stunning aspect about these verses is that the **tree** as well as the **serpent** are both symbols of the goddess Asherah.[21] There is even an etymological connection between the Hebrew name Eve, *hawwah,* and the name Asherah.[22] In addition, there is also a similarity between the name *hawwah* and the Aramaic word *hewya'* for serpent.[23]

Gen. 3:20 The man called his wife's name **Eve,** because she was **the mother of all living.**

---

[19] See the role that desire and vanity play in René Girard's, Mensonge Romantique et Vérité Romanesque, Paris, Grasset, 1961.

[20] "Thus we can see that there is an association between Asherah and trees or symbols related to trees although the full details of this association are unknown. Since Asherah herself is the great mother-goddess, chief consort of the Canaanite high god El, it stands to reason that the cultic symbols of the goddess should be associated with fertility or the gift of life in some manner." See Howard N. Wallace's dissertation, The Eden Narrative, Atlanta, Scholars Press, 114.

[21] Howard N. Wallace, Ibid., 163

[22] "The possible etymologies for *hawwah* suggest that the name and the connection with Asherah are part of a long tradition." Howard N. Wallace, Ibid., 157-158.

[23] Howard N. Wallace, Ibid., 148.

The meaning of Eve as "the mother of all living" is a further allusion to fertility connected to the "mother goddess" Asherah as the "nurse to the gods". Moreover, the explicit consequence of the woman's disobedience is described as the pains of childbearing emphasizing even further the fertility theme of the narrative.

The serpent is a major protagonist in the creation myths of the ancient Near East where he is a celebrated symbol of wisdom.

Mt. 10:16 So be wise as serpents and innocent as doves.

Many of the oldest Egyptian goddesses were thought of as serpents, mostly as cobras. In fact, the symbol of the serpent preceded the name of most of the goddesses and is the hieroglyphic symbol for the word "Goddess". The Sumerian goddess Nidaba, the patron diety of **writing,** was also depicted as a snake, while the Sumerian goddess was referred to as the Great Mother Serpent of Heaven. Furthermore, symbols of numerous goddesses of Old European, Indian, Akkadian, and Babylonian mythologies were also portrayed as serpents. Most of them represented a common symbol of fertility and immortality.[24]

The presence of the snake among God, Adam, and Eve represents the **alien,** which from the outset is excluded from God's design. As such, he is the visible cause of the fall. Furthermore, the narrative correlates the woman to the reptile as both **outsiders.** They are portrayed as the rebellious prototypes who ignore God's command.

As the account shows, the serpent offers Eve much more than the knowledge of good and evil; he tells her she could be God's equal. That suggestion even implies that she would forsake her rank of tiller.

The narrative makes it quite clear that the serpent and the woman are both responsible for man's alienation from God. It is no coincidence that so early in the biblical texts the writers portray the woman and the serpent as being condemned by God. As we mentioned earlier, both are linked to symbols of pagan cults that are radically opposed by Yahweh.

1 Kings 16:32 He erected an altar for Ba'al in the house of Ba'al, which he built in Samar'ia. And Ahab made an Ashe'rah. Ahab

---

[24] Barbara G. Walker, The Woman's Encyclopedia of Myths and Secrets, San Francisco, Harper & Row, 1983, 903-909.

did more to provoke the LORD, the God of Israel, to anger than all the Kings of Israel who were before him.

•

Gen. 3:21 And the LORD God made for Adam and for his wife garments of skins, and **clothed** them. Then the LORD God said, "Behold, the man has become **like** one of **us,** knowing good and evil; and now, lest he put forth his hand and take also of the tree of life, and eat, and live for ever"—therefore the LORD God sent him forth from the garden of Eden, to till the ground from which he was taken. **He drove out the man;** and at the east of the garden of Eden he placed the **cherubim,** and a flaming sword which turned every way, to guard the way to the tree of life.

As a result of the transgression, the couple's eyes were opened and they "perceived" their nakedness.[25] Too much emphasis has been placed on the sexual connotation of the narrative. It is rather the theme of fertility and the nature of **apperception** itself that should be more readily stressed. Their eyes are "opened" to a **new** condition which is closely tied to the transgression. Especially in the awareness of transition from:

nakedness/nature to clothing/culture[26]

The narrative explains that the reason why the woman was enticed to eat the fruit in the first place was to be like God. But as they both ate from the fruit they soon realized that God is the sole ruler of the garden and that they, as tillers, are naked and destitute. As a result, Adam and Eve covered themselves with readily accessible leaves while afterward God clothed them with garments made of skins, denoting the property of cattle. The difference in clothing also marks a distinction between:

leaves/nature and skins/domestication
leaves/agriculture and skins/herdsmanship.

We will see in the next chapter how the exodus is closely tied to the idea of herdsmanship. God himself favored sheepherding, a predominantly patriarchal occupation, over agriculture which

---

[25] Torah, Ibid.

[26] Claude Levi-Strauss, The Raw and the Cooked, New York, Harper & Row, 1969.

was closely connected with the fertility cults of the Goddess which he opposed.

Adam and Eve were living in the garden surrounded by God's overwhelming dominion. Eve, nevertheless, chose to challenge God's authority. She refused to be at the center of God's providential condescension, preferring independence instead. Perhaps the serpent's assertion that the eating of the fruit would not bring her death may have convinced her. In fact, the serpent's assertion turns out to be right, God's threat of impending death does not materialize. It shows here that the serpent is indeed a symbol of wisdom.

Contrary to popular belief, it is not hard work that is the unfortunate consequence of the fall—man tilled and kept the garden before his expulsion—it is the exclusion of man from God's realm. It is an **exclusion** from the presence of the **holy.**

Finally, God is concerned that the couple might also eat from the tree of life and live forever. To eliminate such a prospect he quickly evicts them. The act of disobedience also brought forth suspicion and distrust, another consequence of the fall. Promptly, God places a **cherubim** to guard the garden's entrance. The angel becomes a symbol of man's alienation from God.[27]

As the story shows, the cherub's duty is to guard the boundaries of the **sacred** and to protect the tree of life located at its **center.**

Contrary to popular belief, the cherub—or cherubim—is not a cute and chubby winged child flying about the clouds of heavens. Biblical tradition describes the cherub as a sphinx: a four legged animal often depicted with the body of a lion, the wings of a bird, and the head of a human, most frequently the face of a woman. The cherub was usually carved out of olive wood and plated with gold.[28]

The symbol of the cherub is part of another sacred Jewish tradition. The sphinx was also present inside the first Temple of Jerusalem.[29] Two of these carved creatures were placed side by side with their wings stretched to form the tabernacle. Between their protective custody lay the ark. The ark, which is Israel's most sacred relic, was a golden box which contained the tablets of the ten commandments, and, according to different sources, also contained a

---

[27] The angel, throughout the Bible, is depicted as God's messenger; as such, he is depicted as the symbol of an obstacle to the direct **communication** between God and man.

[28] R.E. Friedman, Ibid., 86-87.

[29] J, who wrote the account, was from the southern kingdom of Judah where Solomon built the first Jerusalem temple. A strict Yahwist, J was outraged by the idolatries of King Jeroboam who ruled the northern kingdom of Israel. The King had built in the cities of Beth-El and Dan two shrines for the worship of the golden calf associated with the fertility cults of Asherah.

sample of the manna; ie, the food sent from heaven to sustain the life of the people of Israel during the exodus.[30]

The symbolic cherub is used as a guardian of both sacred places: the garden of Eden and the ark. At the **center** of the garden are the tree of knowledge of good and evil, and the tree of life. In the midst of the Jerusalem temple, which according to Jewish beliefs is also located at the center of the world, is the ark with the ten commandments and the manna.

Furthermore, the knowledge of good and evil is connected to the law embodied by the ten commandments. One who knows and interprets the law knows the difference between good and evil.

God's immediate concern in placing the cherub is stopping Adam and Eve from eating from the tree of life. Yet the tree of life is also connected to another content of the ark. Both, the tree of life and the manna, are symbols of a sustenance of mysterious origin.

The cherub is put in both places to protect and guard the garden and the ark from the **profane** man and woman. Henceforth, only God is permitted to enter the garden, and only the high priest can enter the Holy of Holies. Jewish law forbids anyone but the priest to enter the Holy of Holies, and whoever does must be killed.

The symbolic analogy between the garden and the ark is interesting. It shows that J, who wrote the account, was preoccupied with preserving the priestly dominion over the divine law. The texts also suggest that the fall brought forth the **separation** between the sacred center which God rules and the outside boundaries of the profane.

•

In the text above, the tree is a metaphor of Asherah, the hidden and profane reality located at the center of the garden. It reveals that the **profane reality** of the **Goddess** has been **excluded** from the sacred texts and the cultic practices of Israel. In the following chapters we will try to show how the opposition to the **profane** reality in general, and to the Goddess in particular, is at the core of the religious experience.

---

[30] Ex. 16:31f.

EXODUS: The God of the Desert

Genesis does not limit itself to the creation narrative. Adam and Eve went on to have children, among them, Cain and Abel. In some respect they typify the consequence of the fall: the evil and the good.

The story of the two brothers is a further allusion to God's preference for herdsmanship over agriculture. Cain's fruit offering is disregarded by God who looked favorably upon Abel's flock offering. As we know, this arouses Cain's jealousy and causes the killing of Abel.

The text goes on with the patriarchal **genealogy** of the first couple's descendants.

As the generations of "men" multiply on earth, it saddens God to see that they are all wicked and evil. As a result, he decides to destroy humankind in a flood. But among the corrupt God finds favor with Noah. He tells him to build an ark in order to save his family and the animals of the earth.

Soon after the flood life begins anew. The narrative goes on with the enumeration of Noah's **descendants.** Meanwhile, the epic of the Patriarchs unfolds. Among the principal heroes are Abraham, Isaac, and Jacob. The narrative depicts successively their own unique relationship with their God.

The saga depicted in Genesis ends with the people of Israel's move to Egypt to escape the famine that ravaged their lands. A fortunate turn of events allows them to be invited to Egypt by Joseph,

Jacob's son, who was sold as a slave to an Egyptian by his jealous brothers. Because of Joseph's uncanny ability to interpret dreams, he had soon been noticed by the Egyptian court and was promoted to a prestigious position among their ranks.

But before we begin with the "epic" of Exodus, Genesis inaugurates three important Old Testament themes:

Abraham .... God's promise and alliance
Isaac .... the spared sacrifice
Jacob .... the struggle with God; ie, Israel

These themes are but a prelude to what is the centerpiece of the Bible: Exodus.

•

Exodus is a unique and invaluable account that discloses the birth of a religion. Everything evolves around the significant experience of the people in the wilderness. In many ways Genesis, which precedes it, simply acts as an introduction to the important excursion of the people of Israel.

The flight out of Egypt and the revelation of Yahweh in the desert are the fundamental points which reveal Israel's origin and identity. The fashion and context in which the journey took place is a remarkable trait that discloses its essence: Moses typifies the semi-nomadic and tribal experience of the "fathers".

The people's isolation in the desert and the transient quality of the journey toward the promised land did not favor the development of a stable culture usually associated with agriculture and the fertility cults of the Goddess. In other words, the unique experience of Israel was a product of its isolation which also gave birth to the exclusive and jealous nature of Yahweh. Being secluded from other gods and cultures favored the unique cult of a single and exclusive God. What followed that experience favored the fierce **opposition** to other gods as well as to the Goddess.

The identity of Israel is, in a sense, closely related to the idea of **flight, movement,** and **seclusion.** The **isolation** of the desert was providential to its historical development where the three entities identified as Moses, Yahweh, and Israel came together in a fateful fashion.

•

Several generations of Hebrews had lived in Egypt since the time of their first arrival. These "people" now felt less and less welcomed in the adoptive land. Their lives were increasingly threatened by oppressive conditions imposed by the Pharaoh.

Among the Egyptians the Hebrews were a "people" without a leader. Moses, it turns out, was a prince without a kingdom. When he is told by God of his destiny on Mount Sinai the revelation links the leader to the people. He saw the apparition and heard God's voice revealing to him the "oath" he made to the Fathers before him.

Israel's identity as a people, as a religion, and as a nation is recreated with that revelation. The exodus in the desert further consolidates that identity. **Apart** and away from the "other" gods and "other" cultures living in Egypt, the setting is favorable for Yahweh to inaugurate a new bond. Yahweh characteristically describes himself as a jealous God, he is unconditionally opposed to "other" gods. As the story shows, the **wilderness** is an ideal place to forge such an alliance.

The introduction begins with the description of Moses' birth. But the "epic" soon shifts to the hierophany. God reveals his presence by the burning bush and the sound of his **voice.** The encounter takes place on Mount Sinai, also called Mount Horeb. According to the traditional lore of the time, the site was, significantly enough, referred to as the "Mountain of God" or the "Mountain of the gods". The sacred place was known locally as an area where mysterious phenomena often occurred. It was commonly believed that divine beings lived there. Coincidentally, the place could not have been more appropriate for Moses' spiritual initiation.[1]

the setting	Egypt and the wilderness
the hero	Moses
the quest	the "promise"
the obstacle	the Pharaoh and other gods
the mentor	Yahweh
the outcome	the ten commandments; Israel

•

The setting underscores the geographical and historical context that led to the exodus. It is an underlying factor in the plot. The spatio-temporal circumstances for Exodus rely on the departure out of Egypt and the movement toward the quest for the promised land.

Exodus is the second book of the Pentateuch. These books are also referred to as the Torah, also known as the Law or Instructions. Early Jewish and Christian traditions believed Moses to be the author of these texts, but biblical scholars discovered that Exodus is not

---

[1] Mountains are privileged places where the sacred appears. See Martin Buber for the Mountain of God in, Moses, Oxford, Phaidon Press Ltd, 109.

the work of one author but rather a compilation of at least four literary sources known as the Yahwist—J, the Elohist—E, the Priestly writer—P, and the Redactor—R. As we have mentioned already, these sources were put together into one narrative by a single editor identified as the Redactor.[2] We will come back to this mysterious editor later.

According to biblical accounts Moses' parents were from the tribe of Levi, one of the many tribes that lived in Egypt. These people were also called the Hebrews. The name "Hebrew" has many etymological origins, and none of them certain. It may have been derived from the word *Habiru,* a variant of *Hapiru* or *Apiru,* which was a designation for a class of people who made their living by offering themselves as hired help. According to biblical tradition, the Israelites had been in Egypt for numerous generations and apparently had become a threat to the Pharaohs because of their ever growing population.[3]

In addition to the Hebrews, there were a great number of slaves from different countries who were brought in as prisoners of war and lived all over Egypt to serve in different capacities. Many became free persons within the Egyptian society and several were found at various levels of rank in the Egyptian court.

Many of these "foreigners" immigrated to Egypt because of its prosperity. As in the case of the Hebrews, some fled the recurrent famines in their own countries. The overwhelming diversity did cause some problems. One document, *The Admonitions of Ipuwer,* conveys the distress felt by the Egyptians by the presence of an increasing number of aliens:

> Foreigners have become people everywhere . . . Robbery is everywhere . . . the desert is [spread] throughout the land . . . Barbarians from outside have come to Egypt . . .[4]

The great number and diversity of these cultures were matched by their respective religious beliefs. Historically though, the Egyptians had been very tolerant of different cults and other gods.

There is little archaeological evidence that corroborates the facts described in Exodus. The Pharaoh in the account, for instance, is not identified. However, we know that the drafting of foreign

---

[2] Richard Elliott Friedman, Who Wrote the Bible, New York, Summit Books, 1987.

[3] Martin Buber, Moses, Ibid., 20.

[4] Ian Wilson, Exodus, The True Story Behind the Biblical Account, San Francisco, Harper & Row, 1985, 56.

labour began with the reign of queen Hatshepsut and her son Thutmose III. The forced labor was later continued by Seti I and Ramses II, *circa* 1300-1225 BC. It is possible that the "Hebrews" were drafted in large number into forced labour for the building of fortified cities on the north-eastern frontier of Egypt. This part of history is nevertheless filled with conjecture. Yet there is one chronicle that depicts the Hebrews suffering at the hands of the Egyptians. The text can be found on the great Rekhmire's tomb who was Thutmose III's vizier. It describes how the Egyptians,

> . . . treated their Israelite slave with ruthless severity . . . setting them to work on clay and brickmaking.[5]

However, the most quoted evidence of the existence of the Hebrews in Egypt is the inscription on a Merneptah stele which reads:

> Israel is desolate, it has no seed left.[6]

As for the period in which the exodus took place, most scholars today support the dating to be around the thirteenth century BC.

Before the exodus the Hebrews, like many other semi-nomadic tribes, had come to Egypt to escape the famine that ravaged their lands. From the time of their arrival in Egypt to the time of their departure the conditions of their lives changed; presumably because of shifts in the policies of the Egyptian monarchy.

From a predominantly agricultural and mercantile society Egypt emerged into a more aggressive militaristic power. The victory over the Hyksos marked the coming to power of a great new dynasty: the Eighteenth. With its fortunes of war Egypt entered a new phase in its history. And the New Kingdom, spanning from 1550 to 1307 BC, is in all probability the setting for Exodus.[7]

•

There is still a lot of debate about the historicity of Moses. There is no clear archaeological evidence proving his existence. Despite this, we cannot deny a "truth of faith" about his character.[8] We

---

[5] Ian Wilson, Ibid., 81. Another clue may be the cities of "Pithom" and "Raam'ses", mentioned in Ex. 1:11, which are known to have been constructed during the reigns of Seti I and Ramses II.

[6] F.F. Bruce, Israel and the Nations, London, The Paternoster Press, 1963, 13.

[7] Ian Wilson, Ibid.

[8] Raffaele Pettazzoni, Essays on the History of Religions, Leiden, Brille, 1967, 21.

cannot dispel either the importance that Moses had on the history of Israel and the development of religion in general.

Curiously, the hero has an "Egyptianized" name which has a twofold etymological origin. On one hand, the name Moses is derived from the Egyptian verb *msy* which means "is born" or "to give birth". The expression could be found in names like Thut-*mose*, meaning "Thoth is Born", and also in Ramses, or Re-*mose*, which means "Re is born". On the other hand, the Hebrew etymology for *Moshe*, associated in Ex. 2:10 with *mashah*, means "drawn out of the water". These two etymological origins bear the dual nature of Moses' ethnical background which is an intrinsic part of his identity.[9]

Acts 7:22 And Moses was instructed in all the wisdom of the Egyptians, and he was mighty in his **words** and deeds.

The narrative begins when Moses' life is providentially saved from the Pharaoh's command to "cast" all the Hebrew newborn males "into the Nile". The Hebrew women had become so fertile that their growing number was viewed as a threat. In order to save Moses from the hands of the infanticide ruler, Moses' parents, Amram and Jochebed, hid their child for three months. When they could not conceal him any longer, his mother put him in a water-tight reed basket and set him afloat on the Nile. The Pharaoh's daughter, while bathing in the river nearby, found the child and recognized him as one of the Hebrew children. Meanwhile, Moses' sister watched her brother's safe destination. She then approached the princess and proposed to let a Hebrew woman nurse the child. Arrangements were made for Moses' mother to nurture the child until he was grown, and then he would be returned to the Pharaoh's daughter.

Mose	*Moshe*
"is born"	"draw out of the water"
Egyptian princess' adoptive son	Hebrew mother

In the course of his life fateful events would confirm Moses' ethnical identity. A determinant episode describes the hero's killing

---

[9] According to S. Freud, Moses was an Egyptian, See Moses and Monotheism, New York, A.A. Knopf, 1939.

of an Egyptian who was beating a Hebrew. As a result, he identified with the plight of his people. But because of his action Moses feared the wrath of the Pharaoh who had heard of the murder, and fled to the Midian desert. His deed made him an **outcast** of the Egyptian society and he was unable to return until the Pharaoh's death.

While he was in the desert he came across a group of women who brought their flock to water at a well. They were the seven daughters of a local tribal priest. As several shepherds attempted to chase them away he came to their rescue. When their father found out about the "Egyptian's" conduct he invited him to share a meal. The dinner apparently went well since the father gave his daughter Zipporah in marriage to Moses. Jethro, the father-in-law, was a Kenite,[10] a tribe reputed for having priests and scribes among its members.

Moses' marriage into the Kenites would prove beneficial for his mission. Priests, particularly scribes, had important roles in royal courts, especially in dealing with the commercial and legal matters of growing tribes and large kingdoms. In that era, the art of writing was closely associated with the scribal and priestly office. Their functions may be compared to the role that accountants play in our society today. These scribes held the highest offices and were part of a privileged caste in the king's court. The knowledge of their craft was closely kept in the family from generation to generation. They acted as clerks who kept records of finances and took inventories of livestock and goods. Rulers depended on them to account for their wealth. In that function they were held in high esteem. In Egypt, scribes were even divinized. Among the first to be honored was Imhotep who was a minister and an architect.[11]

Scribes were legal experts as well. They kept records of alliances and tribal agreements between the sovereigns and their vassals. They performed tasks similar to what lawyers do today. Consequently, the scribes were critical to any potential leader. In these circumstances, Moses' marriage into the Kenites was useful. The priests and scribes of his adopted tribe would be invaluable during the exodus. They helped to consolidate the religious, social, legal, and economical activities of the "people" of Israel. The revelation and then the application of the ten commandments are a perfect example of how the association between the priests and Moses turned out to be essential for the collective management of Israel.

---

[10] He is also called Reu'el in Ex. 2:18 and Hobab in Jg. 4:11. See also Max Weber for more on the scribes and priests in, Ancient Judaism, New York, The Free Press, 1967, 336-343.

[11] Régis Debray, Le Scribe: Genèse du Politique, Paris, Grasset, 1980, 33-36.

●

Until his marriage the hero lived the life of an outcast. But soon, God would call him out of the burning bush to reveal his identity and tell him of his destiny. The primordial encounter establishes the foundation of a triune relationship between Yahweh, Moses, and Israel; ie, God, the leader, and the people.

> Ex. 3:8 ". . . and I have come down to deliver them **out** of the hand of the Egyptians, and to bring them up out of that land to a good and broad land, a land flowing with milk and honey . . ."

Although there is no special term for the word "promise" in the Old Testament, the idea is conveyed by a various range of Hebrew expressions, among them are "speak", "speech", "say", and "swear". Because Yahweh is regarded as the faithful one, His **word** is enough to guarantee the fulfillment of the promise.

The principal term used in Hebrew for land is *'eres.* It is the fourth most used term in the Old Testament. As far as theological interpretation goes, the concepts of land and the covenant are so closely connected that it is almost impossible to describe one without talking about the other. The land is described as Yahweh's gift, which he first promised to Noah, and then to Abraham and his descendants.

Israel was chosen by Yahweh to be his "people for his own possession".[12] The word possession is used in the same manner in which God owns the land. When Yahweh refers to his people he refers to them in terms of his **property.** Herein, the term is used to describe Yahweh's "special" possession of his people in the sense of an acquired property.

The concept of the **promised land** is described in terms of alliance between Yahweh and Israel. The emphasis is laid on the closeness of the relationship between God and his people. God is the owner of the land in the same fashion that he owns his people. And Israel's possession of the land depends on her faithfulness to God. Yahweh as the land-LORD allows the possession of the land by his people only if they remain faithful to his word.

> Lev. 25:23 "The land is mine; for you are strangers and sojourners with me."

---

[12] Deut. 7:6.

•

In the thematic sequence we have identified the Pharaoh as the obstacle that is also closely connected to the gods of Egypt.

Once out of Egypt the Hebrews were free to be Yahweh's chosen people. The narrative goes on to recount the tribulations of their journey in the desert. A particularly crucial episode is described through Moses' outburst of anger when he saw the idolatry of the people as he came down from the presence of God on Mount Sinai. At the sight of the idol, Moses threw and broke the tables of the ten commandments upon the "molten calf". This incident typifies his determination to keep Yahweh's cult free from any foreign influence. This is especially true in the case of the worship of the golden calf. The underlying **antagonism** is fundamental to the whole biblical narrative. This theme may be the key to understanding why "monotheism" has supplanted all other forms of worship in Judaism, especially in connection with the fertility cults of the Goddess.

Ex. 32:8 "These are your gods, O Israel, who brought you up out of the land of Egypt!"

According to the excerpt above, the golden bull-calf is linked to Egypt. But according to E who wrote this account, the "molten calf" relates to a specific episode of heresy that flourished in the cities of Dan and Beth-El in the northern kingdom of Israel during the reign of King Jeroboam to whom E was opposed.

Soon after King Solomon died, the northern kingdom of Israel, under the reign of Jeroboam, seceded from the southern territory of Judah. The division occurred primarily as a result of the unpopular policies of *missim:* a burdensome tax paid in the form of forced labor. Instead of appointing the hereditary priest whose lineage traced back to Moses to the temples in Dan and Beth-El, Jeroboam nominated his own officials for ceremonies related to the golden calf. The "molten calf" was intended to represent the symbolic pedestal as a throne to the invisible Yahweh. But for the great number of Canaanites living in Israel at the time, the golden bull-calf was the visible manifestation of the animal associated with the fertility cult and the goddess Asherah.

It is from this heresy that the whole antagonism to the "molten image" stems. Especially in connection with the Canaanite worship of El and Asherah that we have outlined in the former chapter. The golden calf is also associated by tradition to Baal and her companion Baalat, which could be translated into "lord" or "owner", and "owneress". These cults were popular among the Canaanites who lived in Israel during the time of King Jeroboam. E, who wrote this passage, in all probability lived during the time when these events took place.[13] The account reveals his outrage at Jeroboam for not having appointed a legal priestly heir to the temple to which priestly order E most likely belonged himself.

This is one interpretation of the event. The narrative, however, links the worship of the "molten calf" to Egypt.

If we go along with the story and believe that the golden calf really originated in Egypt, then we might try to find parallels of the golden calf in Egyptian religion.

Several scholars believe that Ramses II and his son Menerptah were the probable oppressors of the Hebrew people.[14] When Ramses II made peace with the Hittites following the disastrous battle of Kadesh, a great number of deities such as **Anat, Astarte,** and **Asherah** became popular in Egypt. Archaeological findings show that the Canaanite gods, particularly the goddesses, had an extraordinary "fluidity" in taking the shapes, forms, and names of other deities.[15] This is especially the case in warfare and conquest where acculturation becomes widespread among the different cultures and the divinities assume the identity of other gods. This is the case in regards to the Canaanite goddesses Asherah, or Astarte, and her Near Eastern counterpart Anath.

There were numerous bull cults in ancient Egypt, most of them minor divinities. Among them were, the black Apis Bull, the white Min Bull, a symbol of virility, and Mont-Re. But none of these cults was more important than the one portrayed by the cow-goddess. This divinity was found in a very early stage of Egyptian religion and became prevalent throughout Egypt. The most famous cow-goddess was Hathor. One of the more popular goddesses in Egypt, Hathor was a sky-goddess and a symbol of fertility. As the sky-goddess, she was the Eye of the Sun god Re. In that quality, she personified the sky. She was known as the Beautiful One and the **Golden One**; the joyous goddess of love, music, and happiness. Gold was her sacred metal and Hathor was described as the "Gold of the

---

[13] Ex. 32:1 to 33:1.

[14] It is believed that during his long reign—1301 to 1234 BC—Ramses II ordered the construction of numerous temples with colossal statues of gods and of himself. The four deities behind his temple at Abu Simbel show that he was placing himself at the same level as the three dynastic gods of Egypt: Ptah, Re, and Amon. It is during the successive reign of his son Menerptah—1234-27 BC—that we have the famous inscription about Israel: "Israel is desolate; it has no seed left."

[15] William Foxwell Albright, Archaeology and the Religion of Israel, Baltimore, The Johns Hopkins Press, 1968, 71 f.

Gods". She was also called "the Lady of the Sycamore". As we have seen in the former chapter the tree is also the symbol of Asherah. Hathor was especially popular among women. She incarnated the principles of beauty, love, and fertility. As such, she typified the Mother Goddess. Hathor was especially concerned with birth and babies. As a "cow" she suckled the baby kings and protected them through childhood. Her protection even extended to kings in their old age. Throughout Egyptian history, the Golden One remained a very popular goddess.[16]

There are some striking similarities between the golden calf from Exodus and the Golden One, the goddess of fertility. In addition, the reference in the text to the "play" and the "sound of singing" among the worshippers when Moses came down from Mount Sinai points to an additional likeness between the two deities. Hathor was the bringer of happiness, and the goddess of music and love.

The "molten calf", however, was dealt a hard blow by Moses. Yahweh is indeed a jealous God. He allows no other God but himself. Following Moses' destruction of the idol, the worshippers who did not repent were all killed by the faithful Levite priests. Loyal to their functions, they made sure the worship of the forbidden image would be completely eradicated.

> Ex. 20:3 "You shall have **no other gods** before me. You shall not make for yourself a graven image, or any likeness of anything that is in heaven above . . . for I the LORD your God am a **jealous** God . . ."

•

The narrative is particularly explicit about Moses' inquiry of God's identity. The name that is revealed to Moses, Yahweh—YHWH in the unvocalized Hebrew—is so sacred in Jewish tradition that it is not pronounced; instead, God, Adonai, El Shaddai, or the LORD is regularly substituted for it.

Ex. 3:14 "I AM WHO I AM"
"Ehyeh-asher-ehyeh"

As Martin Buber points out, God's name is not meant to be esoteric.[17] It is not made to avoid any question about God's identity

---

[16] See, Barbara Watterson, The Gods of Ancient Egypt, New York, Facts On File Publication, 1984.

[17] M. Buber, Ibid., 192-195.

or to withhold any information about his being. Instead, the twofold *ehyeh*—I am—implies God's **presence** and closeness with whom he has chosen. In fact, Yahweh is so close to Moses that he is his "mouth":

Ex. 4:12 "Now therefore go, and I will be with your mouth and teach you what you shall speak."

Furthermore, as we have already seen in the first verses of Genesis, God is once again an *individuum vaguum,* the imageless voice speaking out of nowhere. Yahweh's revelation to Moses is also meant to be the "sign" or a visible expression of God's presence. When Yahweh asks Moses to say to the people of Israel: "I AM has sent me to you", God literally implies his overwhelming presence in Moses. His mouth is Yahweh's mouth. Moses is the "sign" sent by Yahweh.

Ex. 3:12 He said, "But I will be with you; and this shall be the **sign** for you, that I have sent you:"

Therefore, the essence of the **name** of God becomes in effect secondary, since the name merely underlines God's presence; the God of the Fathers is present with Moses as he was present with Abraham, Isaac, and Jacob. Yahweh is present with Moses as the historical manifestation of God's promise he made to the Patriarchs. God's revelation to Moses is made in order to deliver the Israelites from their bondage in Egypt.

The "I AM WHO I AM" becomes clearer in conjunction with Moses' realization of his identity as the spokesman. He is the historical manifestation of Yahweh's promise made to Israel. The same promise he made to Abraham is related to Moses; yet, according to Yahweh, it is the first time his name has been revealed.

Yahweh is Moses' mentor. Moses is chosen by Yahweh to embody the verbal promise. However, Moses needs additional help in his mission. Aaron, his brother, becomes the heroe's spokesman in his dealings with the Pharaoh. In the text God commands Moses to "Say to Aaron".[18] The reason being that Moses, who has some kind of speech impediment and may have been a stammerer, is inflicted with such a dread to speak to the Pharaoh that he refuses to obey God's command. He argues stubbornly with God and arouses his anger. Yahweh finally agrees to let Moses' brother be

---

[18] Ex. 7:19; 8:5; 16.

42

his spokesman. Aaron, in effect, becomes Moses' "mouth" in the same fashion that Moses is Yahweh's "mouth".

Further help is needed for the favorable outcome and the final release of the people from Egypt. The plagues are an additional and necessary force to convince the Pharaoh of God's will. Yahweh uses the plagues as a powerful **sign** to break the ruler's obstinacy. One at a time, the plagues are announced by Moses through Aaron. The account of the plagues are for the most part ornamental. They symbolize Yahweh's control over nature, since Moses does not have the Pharaoh's military might.[19]

The plagues: 1) the water into blood
                2) the frogs
                3) the gnats
                4) the flies
                5) the murrain
                6) the boils
                7) the hail
                8) the locusts
                9) the darkness
               10) the death of the first-born
                        •

The outcome of Exodus is profiled by the quest of the **promised** land. As we will see, what is at issue here is as much the quest underlined by the "promise" as the actual possession of the **land** itself.[20]

But as we get closer to the denouement, Moses is faced with a dilemma. He is concerned about the future of the people's faithfulness to Yahweh. The Israelites, in the course of their exodus, lived a nomadic way of life and the relationship between Yahweh and his people thrived in the desert. The idea of a fixed settlement in Canaan puts an end to those ideal conditions. In the wilderness God took care of his people, guiding them like a shepherd that brings his cattle to grazing lands. There is a certain amount of nostalgia

---

[19] The last plague, the one that finally convinces the Pharaoh to release the Israelites, may have an underlying significance that is of some interest. There is a parallel between the Pharaoh's killing of the Hebrew male infants in the beginning of the narrative, from which Moses escapes, and the death of all the Egyptian first-born including the ailing Pharaohs' child (Ex. 11:1-12). The meaning of the last plague can be related to "blood revenge" of the ancient customs of the Semitic tribes: "eye for eye, tooth for tooth" (Ex. 21:24, Deut. 19:21, Mt. 5:38), described in the law of retribution of the Covenant Code. See Max Weber, Ancient Judaism, New York, Macmillan Co., Inc., 1967, 61-62.

[20] In Hebrew the word for covenant is *berith*. It has the same significance as bond or agreement. Many social relationships of the time were agreements also known as covenants between Kings.

and preoccupation at the end of the journey as to the future of this unique relationship. In the promised land the people would no longer live in the isolation of the desert with one God, as one people, but among foreign cultures and alien gods.

> Deut. 7:1 "When the LORD your God brings you into the land which you are entering to take possession of it, and clears away many nations before you, the Hittites, the Gir'gashites, the Amorites, the Canaanites, the Per'izzites, the Hivites, and the Jeb'usites, seven nations greater and mightier than yourself, and when the LORD your God gives them over to you, and you defeat them; then you must utterly destroy them; you shall make no covenant with them, and show no mercy to them. You shall not make marriages with them, giving your daughters to their sons or taking their daughters for your sons. For they would turn away your sons from following me, to serve other gods; then the anger of the LORD would be kindled against you, and he would destroy you quickly. But thus shall you deal with them: you shall break down their altars, and dash in pieces their pillars, and hew down their **Ashe'rim,** and burn their graven images with fire.
> "For you are a people holy to the LORD your God; the LORD your God has chosen you to be a people for his own possession, out of all the peoples that are on the face of the earth."

It is paradoxical, in these circumstances, that Moses will never set foot in Canaan, the land he yearned for so long. Only the people of Israel led by Joshua will.

Canaan was populated by natives who worshipped different gods. Unlike in the isolation of the desert, Yahweh would be surrounded by other gods. Among the people living there were the Canaanites who, as we have already outlined, were worshippers of Asherah, the goddess of fertility.

History reveals that the people would eventually intermarry with their Canaanite neighbors and be influenced by the settled and agricultural ways of life associated with fertility cults, despite the evils associated with agriculture and the slavery suffered in Egypt which are vilified in Exodus.[21]

Once settled in the promised land, Yahweh's exclusivity was

---

[21] See Michael Walzer, Exodus and Revolution, New York, Basic Books, 1985, 101. Also Deut. 11:10.

forever threatened. The danger was always present that the people of Israel would forgo and forget their bond with Yahweh. A worrisome and perhaps challenging prospect for God and his prophets. More so, for the scribes and priests who wrote these texts.

The **antagonism** of Yahweh to any other form of worship is fundamental to Israel. Yet it is an underlying principle of all religious reality. The greater the opposition to other gods, the closer the relationship with God. The stronger the antagonism between Yahweh and the other cults, the stronger Israel's religious identity. The stronger the identity, the greater the belief, etc.

sacred	vs	*profane*
Yahweh	vs	Asherah
one God	vs	other gods/goddesses

The journey out of Egypt is the beginning of Israel as a people and as a religion. And the revelation of Yahweh on mount Sinai inaugurates the worship of an **exclusive** God. Although there was no word in biblical times for "religion", the beliefs associated with the entity of God, his Kings, priests, prophets, and his people were perceived as one single reality.

This was made possible by the covenant that Yahweh made with the Patriarchs and, finally, with Moses. What begun in Exodus is promulgated by faith and verified by history, notably in the "story". For Israel, the self-fulfilling **words** of God are tied to the faith in the unfolding events of history which are related to Exodus. The covenant sealed the destiny of Israel to the **promise.** The "ultimate concern" lies in the hope that the exclusive alliance will not fade with time. Attached to the covenant is the unbreakable character of the relationship that is stressed upon Israel in the form of the ten commandments and the **law.**[22]

With the law, Exodus inaugurates the legal, the social, and the "religious" aspect of Israel as an inseparable reality. Under **one** God Israel becomes **one** entity, **one** identity.

Another paradox is that Yahweh must rely on his people's obedience as much as they on his guidance. Without his people Yahweh could not survive, and for that matter he would not exist. There-

---

[22] The wilderness period was the constitutional age, the time of Israel's beginning, the time when God's commandments were made into law. In Exodus—Ex. 34:28, Deut. 4:13, 10:4—the term "ten words" has been replaced by the more common appellation of the "ten commandments". The expression "ten words" refers to a group of prescriptions of cultic nature. It is used in the OT to describe a group of divine commandments written down by Yahweh and given to Moses.

fore, Israel is the chosen people of Yahweh as much as Yahweh is their chosen God. This exclusive alliance sets the people **apart** from other people as much as Yahweh is set **apart** from other gods.

But in the outcome, the law and the "word" become the ultimate legacy and the monopoly of the priestly hierarchy. The divine ordinances regulate and keep the community together. With the liturgy, the cults, and the rituals, the priesthood becomes the ruling order of religion. In effect, "man" is under the priest's regulatory supervision for his access to God. The hierarchy of the sacred becomes the medium through which "man" can have access to the holy.

> Ex. 19:5 "Now therefore, if you will obey my voice and keep my covenant, you shall be **my own possession** among all peoples; for all the earth is mine, and you shall be to me a kingdom of **priests** and a **holy** nation."

Exodus illustrates literally how the "story", or the creative power of the **word** as outlined in Genesis, is the creative agent of Israel's identity and history. In fact, the historicity of Exodus is not as important as the "truth of faith" that generates the actual belief of its own sacredness.[23]

· · ·

As we have explained, Exodus stems from four different literary sources: E, J, P, and R which were edited by the Redactor. The first three sources were written much later than the actual exodus, most likely between 922 and 608 BC. And the Redactor, in all probability, compiled the texts during the fourth century BC, more than eight centuries after the actual events described in Exodus took place. It would be revealing at this stage, to find out more about this elusive character who is responsible for the compilation of the most important book ever written in Christendom.

If we were to gather all the data available concerning the identity of this obscure and uncelebrated editor, we would probably end up with a portrait that would look a lot like Ezra.

In 587 BC, the southern kingdom of Judah was defeated by the Babylonians and its inhabitants were sent into exile. The city of Jerusalem was devastated and the temple destroyed. Providentially, Babylon was later conquered by the Persian king Cyrus in 539 BC. He apparently had no religious beliefs of his own and he did not

---

[23] The most revered and holy place for the Israelites during their exodus was the tabernacle, inside which the ark contained the copy of the sacred tablets containing the ten commandments. Again the legacy of the written "word" remains the most sacred religious reality for posterity, handed down from generation to generation.

particularly care to impose any creed upon others. He allowed the Jews to return to their land and worship their God. With his assistance, a second temple was built in 515 BC. Not surprisingly, the king was hailed as the right hand of Yahweh and a good shepherd.

Ezra 1:1 The LORD stirred up the spirit of Cyrus king of Persia.

With the new temple being built, hope was on the rise. Under the new Persian rule, a Jewish exile called Nehemiah was appointed as the civil governor of Jerusalem. He needed additional help in religious matters, so he asked for another official from the Persian courts. This man was Ezra. He was a priest of Aaronid descent who was described as the "Secretary of State for the Jewish Affairs", and the "scribe of the law of the God in heaven". The reference of "God in heaven" was a title commonly given to Yahweh by the Persian regime.

Ezra came with a specific goal: to put religious order among the ruins of Jerusalem and Israel.

He did not come empty handed. He brought with him the copy of an intriguing law-book, which in all likelihood was a copy of the Pentateuch as we know it today. Not surprisingly, Ezra stands out at the end of the Pentateuchal law of the Old Testament in the same fashion as Moses stands at the beginning of it. He was presumably a man of great authority. As such he applied the law scrupulously and with great discipline.

Ezra 7:6 He was a scribe skilled in the law of Moses which the LORD the God of Israel had given.

Upon his arrival in Judah, he was struck by the religious heresy of the Jewish people. He soon forbid the common practice of intermarriage between Jews and their non-Jewish neighbors. He even persuaded already married Jews to divorce their Gentile consorts.

Neh. 9:2 And the Israelites **separated** themselves from all foreigners, and stood and confessed their sins and the iniquities of their fathers.

Religious laxity had spread among the Jews during the Babylonian rule. Apathy for their God was adamant. During the exile, numerous communities who were scattered all over the Babylonian empire had turned their back to the scrupulous observances demanded by Yahweh. While the temple of Jerusalem lay in ruins,

Jewish communities in Egypt and elsewhere lost their urge to worship Yahweh as the law demanded. *Loin des yeux loin du coeur*—far from sight the heart grows distant.

Worse yet the name of Yahweh was freely associated with the goddess Anath, whose identity is closely related to Asherah and Astarte, names that are repeatedly interchanged in the Bible.

The reference to "the queen of heaven" mentioned in the quote below shows how popular the worship of the goddess Asherah had become. When the people were exhorted by the prophet to return exclusively to Yahweh, a group of women retorted:

> Jer. 44:16 "As for the word which you have spoken to us in the name of the LORD, we will not listen to you. But we will do everything that we have vowed, burn incense to the **queen of heaven** and pour out libations to her, as we did, both we and our fathers, our kings and our princes, in the cities of Judah and in the streets of Jerusalem; for then we had plenty of food, and prospered, and saw no evil. But since we left off burning incense to the **queen of heaven** and pouring out libations to her, we have lacked everything and have been consumed by the **sword** and by famine."

Ezra was understandably outraged to see Yahweh rivaled by the **profane reality** of the Goddess. More so to hear such profanity. He took upon himself to forcefully inaugurate a temple-state "hierocracy".[24] He put the temple of Jerusalem back at the center of Jewish religion just as it was before. Patriarchal order was soon restored. The priestly monopoly of the law was reinstated.

Herein lies the background of the Bible.

For ages it was believed that the Pentateuch was written by Moses. Even today some still believe it. It only goes to show what a great job the redactor did when he arranged the different sources together.

What is so amazing is how successfully he put into a single narrative often contradictory accounts. A close scrutiny of the text, however, reveals some important discrepancies between the different sources. In J's account, for instance, God personally descends on Mount Sinai, while in P's God does not. In both J's and E's Moses sees God, not in P's. J and E repeatedly describe Yahweh as merciful

---

[24] F.F. Bruce, Ibid., 109

whereas P never uses the word "mercy", but describes the LORD as the God of justice and anger.

To make matters worse, the different sources challenged each other's priestly authority. E backs the Levitical priestly family of Shiloh, and J is a patron of the descendants of Zadok. Whereas, P and R are supporters of the Aaronide lineage who are openly critical of Moses.

Why then, did the Redactor put these contradictory accounts together? Probably because each individual text was considered sacred and popular among the segment of the population from which it emerged.

In addition to his editorial savvy, R was also an astute theologian. By arranging different versions into one single account, he leaves the final authority regarding matters of theological interpretation to the priestly office. No single truth can be asserted. Every aspect can be challenged by a contradictory version. Therefore, any interpretation of the text can always be questioned, leaving the monopoly of **authority** in matters of faith in the hands of the priesthood.

•

It is one of the greatest paradox of Exodus that Moses did not set foot on the promised land. Yet this paradox may confirm an underlying principle of religious experience: that the **quest** is the essence of belief, not the object itself. In other words, it is the expectation and hope rather than the fulfillment of the promise that is the essence of faith. The promised land is the metaphor for the quest.

Another important principle lies in the **obstacle** to the quest. An underlying **opposition** to the **profane reality** of other god(s) and goddess(es) must be enforced in order to maintain the exclusivity of the **holy.** Concurrently, when God changes Jacob's name to Israel, he reveals a fundamental tenet of the religious reality:

> Gen. 32:28 Then he said, "Your name shall no more be called Jacob, but **Israel,** for you have **striven** with God and with men, and have prevailed."

Israel literally means "He who **strives** with God" or "God **strives".** Hence the very essence of the word Israel lies in the **antagonism** to the **profane reality** of the **other** god(s) and goddess(es) in order to fortify its sacred identity.

JOB:
The Hero's
Vision;
A Profane
Experience

Exodus recounts the story of the journey in the desert, where God sets **apart** his people from other people and where the people reciprocally **separate** Yahweh from other gods. In the Book of Job, however, the hero is temporarily **alienated** from his God and undertakes a journey into the **profane** where he is totally **segregated** from the world. Both narratives are excursions into the unknown. Both disclose a revelation of God.

•

The narrative tells the story of an upright man whose integrity is put to the test. The hero is chastised and tormented for no apparent reason. All along, he insists on his innocence and pleads for justice. But before he is finally restored to a greater glory, he is completely excluded from his God, friends, and community. He becomes the outcast of outcasts. He is the innocent victim repudiated by the whole society.

the setting	the land of Uz
the hero	Job
the quest	justice
the obstacle	Satan
the mentor	Job's integrity
the outcome	the sight of God

The "Book of Job" is called *Iyyov* in Hebrew. The etymology of the word may have meant originally "enemy", while a similar Arabic root signifies "the penitent".

The form and themes of the narrative are closely similar to the Babylonian wisdom writings of the "Poem of the Righteous Sufferer"—XIVth century BC—and the "Acrostic Dialogue on Theodicy"—IXth century BC. It also bears some resemblance to the Egyptian texts called "The Complaints of the Eloquent Peasant" and "Dialogue of the Man Weary of his Life and Soul", both written between the XXth and the XVIIIth century BC.

The author is unknown. The date of the book is uncertain, but popular consensus points to dates ranging between 600-400 BC.

Job is a man from the land of Uz, a place somewhere at the edge of the desert, in the south-eastern parts of the Dead Sea; probably a city of ancient Edom.

Outline and content:

I. The prologue (1:1-2:13)
   A. Job's happiness (1:1-5)
   B. Job is tested (1:6-2:13)
      1. Satan accuses Job (1:6-12)
      2. Job's integrity in his loss of family and property (1:13-22)
      3. Satan's second accusation (2:1-6)
      4. Job's integrity in personal suffering (2:7-10)
      5. the coming of the friends (2:11-13)

II. The dialogues (3:1-41:34)
   A. Job curses the day of his birth (3:1-26)
   B. The first series of the speeches (4:1-14:22)
      1. Eliphaz (4:1-5:27)
      2. Job's reply (6:1-7:21)
      3. Bildad (8:1-22)
      4. Job's reply (9:1-10:22)
      5. Zophar (11:1-20)
      6. Job's reply (12:1-14:22)
   C. The second series of speeches (15:1-21:34)
      1. Eliphaz (15:1-35)
      2. Job's reply (16:1-17:16)
      3. Bildad (18:1-21)
      4. Job's reply (19:1-29)
      5. Zophar (20:1-29)

The central theme of the narrative is set on the theological debate about God's divine right not to justify his actions to "man". His authority is enough of a prerogative to sanction any of his deeds. And, no matter how unjust his actions may appear, they should not be questioned by man since God is God.

●

Job is not an Israelite; he is depicted in the narrative as a **foreigner**. His life is described as being exemplar. We might say that he is a perfect mythical model:

Job 1:8 "Have you considered my servant Job, that there is none like him on the earth . . ."

His life is blessed with numerous children, and he is surrounded my many loyal servants. His wealth is measurably abundant with cattle.

Job 1:3 . . . this man was the greatest of all the people of the east.

Nevertheless, Job is unaware that in the highest courts his integrity is being questioned and his livelihood is at stake.

One day, the sons of God appear at his court accompanied by a stranger. Curious about the newcomer, God asks him of his whereabouts. Satan, without being specific, replies that he roamed the earth. God must have presumed the intruder wise since he questions him about Job's righteousness. Satan's response is that Job has no merit for his probity since he has been favored by the LORD's grace. God, to prove Satan's allegations wrong, allows Job to be put to a test. As a result, Job loses his wealth and his children die. Job is distraught, but he remains loyal to his God. His character remains intact. Unfortunately, Satan does not give up. He returns a second time and insists that Job will curse God's name if he takes his good health away. Again, the LORD allows the fiend to inflict a terrible disease on Job:

Job 2:7 . . . loathsome sores from the sole of his foot to the crown of his head.

Overtaken by his infliction, Job admits having sinned in his life but proclaims that his punishment is outrageously disproportionate to his offense.

Despite the calamities that befall him, he refuses to curse his God. He even remains steadfast against his wife's incessant plea to damn his creator for his unjust treatment. Despite all, Job remains true to his Lord. But when a group of his friends come to deplore his condition, Job's willpower begins to falter. He finally curses the day that he was born.

The long series of dialogues and lamentations begin. His friends, instead of lending their support, condemn him. They maintain that he must be guilty to deserve such a fate, since God is just.

•

Before his ordeal, Job was living content unaware that God was willing to forsake him in order to test his integrity.

As the calamities befall him one after the other, our hero cries for **justice,** unaware of what his dreadful experience is about to reveal.

•

Contrary to Genesis, where the serpent entices the woman to challenge God's command, the narrative presents Satan as the one who defies the LORD to test Job's integrity. Satan is presented as a symbol of wisdom, since he has roamed the earth, and God is curious to know his opinion about his prized servant.

Nothing is said about the alien except that he is not one of God's sons. Etymologically, the word Satan in Hebrew means **adversary.** It is synonymous with **accuser** or **prosecutor.**[1] It also entails one who takes up an **antagonistic** position against somebody; ie, an **enemy.**[2]

What follows is perplexing. God forsakes his favorite servant at the suggestion made by a stranger. As a result, Job becomes a **scapegoat** of God's inscrutable design.

As the afflictions haunt our hero, everybody, from the highest rank to the lowest cast, begins to avoid and shun him.

Plagued by a horrible disease and bad breath, his wife finds him repulsive. Even his servants treat him as a stranger. Children everywhere despise him. His intimate friends abhor him. He is even reviled by the outcasts of the community. He is singled out as a scapegoat and totally excluded from society. God's favorite servant has become a pariah rejected by the whole community.

His friends, instead of consoling him, ask him to repent for his sins, since God rewards the just and punishes the guilty. Therefore, Job should repent.

Such is the subject of all the dialogues between Job and his friends Eliphaz, Bildad, Zophar, and Elihu.

They symbolize the ''order'' in society. They, like Job before his downfall, are all representatives of the hierarchy, they are delegates of the status quo. They rally to God's side to preserve the order of which they are a part. They hold on to the belief that God rewards the righteous by giving him wealth and power, alternatively punishing the sinner by taking away his riches and making him an outcast. God is an ally of the strong. He selects the upright and blameless and segregates the offender.

Their biggest fear, it seems, is that the hero's downfall might portend their own demise if they don't sanction God's condemnation. Therefore, like a contagious disease, he must be quarantined.

---

[1] Zech. 3:1-5 and I Chr. 21:1. Paul in Romans 16:20, equates the serpent of Genesis to the Satan of Job. The reptile, symbol of the Goddess and fertility in the creation myth, is held responsible in Job for the alienation between God and ''man''.

[2] The Arabic verb for *Shatana* also means ''to be remote'', especially from the truth of God.

As a result, the process of collective victimization begins. It is focused on a sole victim: the **scapegoat**. As they all rally to God's decision, Job is singled out to safeguard against the divine wrath. The ostracism becomes in effect a "violent" process of social segregation. Not only Job's friends but all the members of the community behave in a "mimical" fashion. They aggregate into a dynamic entity—a "mob"—whose sole purpose is to foment a consensus against their chosen victim and exclude him from their ranks. Job is chosen precisely as the scapegoat for an ultimate purpose: to defend the order and hierarchy of society which the victim is believed to be threatening.[3]

Yet it is the complete exclusion from society that enables Job to experience his revelation. It allows him to perceive the whole reality of God and of the community from which he becomes **excluded**. Because he is segregated, he sees social reality as an **outsider**. He perceives the whole structure of the society from without.

As the hero finally survives his ordeal, he is reinstated with greater power and glory than he previously had. The mythological significance disclosed in the account is central: the dynamic interaction between the hero, as an **individual,** and God and society becomes the foundation of the revelation.[4]

It goes without saying that the **journey** is an arduous one. Similar, in some respects, to Israel's experience in the desert: a trek into the unknown. And although Satan is depicted as the obstacle, he nevertheless plays a primordial part in the development of the hero's apperception of God.

•

Even though the process of victimization is painful for Job, it is necessary in order for him to see God. To this effect the mentor is Job's **integrity** itself. His trial shows how his personal righteousness is essential to the final outcome. It enables him to transcend his perception of God's reality. Job's wisdom allows him to recognize that his personal rectitude is not justifiable in the face of God. God's authority, albeit a questionable one, is still a divine prerogative. God has a theological precedence over humans, and Job is no exception no matter how righteous he is.

The text describes him as "blameless" and "upright", he fears God and turns away from evil. His integrity, however, does not imply

---

[3] See René Girard, Job: the Victim of his People, London, Athlone Press, 1967, and his other work, The Scapegoat, Chicago, Johns Hopkins University Press, 1986. See also the interesting analysis made by Dabrowski Kazimierz about desintegration, in, Positive Desintegration, Boston, Little, Brown, 1964.

[4] As René Girard puts it "religion is in itself culture" Ibid. Job, 152.

that he is sinless. His uprightness is used in the sense of his perfect integration into the community and with the environment rather than his being without sin.

Furthermore, Job's integrity implies that his personality is **whole** and that he is at peace with himself and with his community. His relationships are of the ''right'' kind with his family, and with his God. This righteousness translates itself into peace— *shalom*—and well being.

This quality is in turn transmitted to his progeny. His sense of responsibility is such that he even performs atonement for his sons in anticipation that they might commit blasphemy.

Job's piety is only matched by his virtue. In the Book of Job, adversity meets integrity head on and integrity is not subdued.

•

We have already outlined that the denouement is revealed in terms of a vision of God. The journey reveals what is at the core of the religious **experience.**[5]

The focal point in any definition of religion revolves around the nature and function of the **sacred.** It is the matrix of any religious phenomenon whatever its cultural or historical origin. Emile Durkheim showed the importance of the dichotomy between the sacred and the profane.[6] The sacred generates a field of belief unto itself which is best defined in terms of **conviction.** Nothing in particular is sacred yet anything can be sacred. It all depends on the historical or the spatio-temporal circumstances under which a certain phenomenon becomes sacrosanct. That is what is referred to as a **hierophany:** namely, when the sacred manifests itself in history as typified by Yahweh and the burning bush. And when the sacred appears, it automatically imposes an arbitrary distance to the **profane,** which it opposes.

sacred	vs	*profane*
''holy ground''	vs	the common ground
Yahweh	vs	the other gods
the center	vs	the outside

---

[5] This experience is recounted in myth, yet it is only an **expression** of the experience, and it must be differentiated from the religious experience itself, which is unique and unfathomable and cannot be properly described in words because they convey only a glimpse of the religious experience. Consequently, we can only rely on the **language** that relates that experience.

[6] Emile Durkheim, The Elementary Forms of the Religious Life, New York, Free Press, 1965 and Rudolf Otto, in, The Idea of the Holy, London, Oxford University Press, 1958.

Normally, God is the Holy One. Yet, in the narrative, he shares his sacredness with his favorite servant. As Satan explains,

> Job 1:10 "Hast thou not put a hedge about him . . . on every side?"

In other words, Job has been overwhelmingly protected and favored by God. He has been put at the **center** of God's holy embrace.

The sacred claims the supremacy of attention. It also attempts to circumscribe a reality, more precisely, an identity. And this identity is maintained by its opposition to the profane. The sacred is by definition that which is distinct from the profane. However, the profane is a religious reality necessary to the sacred, since the sacred is sacred precisely because of its opposition to the profane. Satan, as the **adversary,** illustrates very well what we mean. Satan is Satan because he instigates the conflict between God and Job. He separates the holy union between the LORD and his servant, propelling Job into the realm of the profane where he is excluded from everything.

The following illustrates how the profane plays a critical role in the edification of the sacred:

holy/sacred	vs	common/profane
Moses/Israel	vs	Pharaoh/Egypt
Yahweh	vs	the **other** gods and goddesses

As noted by Mircea Eliade, the dynamic relation between the sacred and the profane demonstrates that anything can be consecrated.[7] It is not specific persons or things that have sacred values *per se,* it is because they are recognized as such at some crucial moment in time. The epiphany of the burning bush, for instance, has been **consecrated** by the **narrative** as the ultimate revelation of Yahweh and has been acknowledged as such by the "people" of Israel.

The sacred always imposes a **separation** and a distance between its center, depicted as holy, and the profane, located outside its periphery. Hence, the profane, which lies beyond the consecrated field, is depicted as the excluded and the alien.

The dichotomy between these two principles is an essential one. Just think of the division between:

---

[7] Mircea Eliade, The Sacred and the Profane, New York, Harper & Row, 1959.

sacred	vs	profane
God/good	vs	Satan/evil
Jews	vs	Gentiles
Christians	vs	the heathen, the pagan
Muslims	vs	the infidels

Furthermore, all religious creeds underline an opposition to the **outside** world defined as the profane. Our **world** is meaningful, while the **other** world is chaotic and mostly inhabited with strangers also described as demons.[8] As outlined in the Book of Job, Satan is a foreigner and an alien.

Literally the word profane means "that which is outside the temple". The profane refers to whatever lies beyond the boundaries of the sacred. This explains why the profane is never cited in clear terms. By definition, the outside world is always **other:** a blurred reality always inhabited by unknown and strange beings. As such, it is perceived as a threat to the vivid reality of the sacred to which we identify. Yet this other reality is threatening precisely because it presents an-**other** sacred reality of its own that challenges the exclusivity of our beliefs. In other words, this other reality defies the foundation of the exclusive validity of our sacred beliefs. Therefore, our beliefs are defined as sacred and are opposed to other beliefs described as alien which are ruled by other gods. Our mythical cosmos confines us to recognize only our world as sacred and discard the rest as profane.

Religion generates its sacred identity from the myths and rituals that perpetuate the creed regulated by the hierarchy of priests. The closer one is to the "holy", the greater the sense of sacredness. Hence, the antagonism amplifies the identities of the sacred and the profane. The stronger the opposition the stronger the belief in the sacred.

sacred	vs	profane
believers	vs	unbelievers
theists	vs	atheists
civilized	vs	primitive

Belief is generated by the dynamic opposition between the two principles. As the Bible shows, the God of the fathers must be protected against the intrusion of other gods that might challenge His

---

[8] Roger Caillois, L'Homme et le Sacré, Paris, Gallimard, 1939, 35-59.

supremacy. Therefore, we always acknowledge the sacred validity of our own religious beliefs but deny it to others.

This is one of the reasons why the profane is always excluded from the sacred. Because it challenges the foundation of the absolute validity of the sacred and it shatters the conviction in the religious uniqueness of the sacred and its tenets.

To protect this supremacy, the sacred precipitates the dynamic opposition to keep the profane at a distance. This is why the essence of faith lies in **antagonism:**

> Gen. 32:28 "Your name shall no more be called Jacob, but **Israel,** for you have **striven** with God and with men, and have prevailed."

We find this dichotomy in each and every religion. What is viewed as sacred is opposed to the profane which in turn has a sacred validity of its own. In other words, the sacred seeks to be exclusive while denigrating the profane's own sacred validity.

•

Job has been described as "the greatest of all people in the east", protected by God's grace and surrounded by his sacred embrace. As the story unfolds, we witness Job's downfall. Originally at the center of attention, he becomes more and more alienated from God and the community. As he becomes **excluded,** he is also debased. The hero is singled out as victim and scapegoat. Finally, he is isolated from the very society in which he was a central figure.

As Job loses everything, he is further segregated into the realm of the **profane.** Formerly at the center of God's favor, he now stands isolated from everybody, outside of the LORD's reach. As such, he lives the life of a total outcast. He becomes the prototype of a **lord-victim.**

> Job 3:20 "Why is light given to him that is in misery,
>   and life to the bitter in soul,
>   who long for death, but it comes not,
>   and dig for it more than for hid treasures;

•

Closely related to the sacred and the profane is a third concept which is essential to the whole dynamic religious experience. This principle is the **wholly other.**[9]

---

[9] Rudolph Otto, Ibid., 25.

The term **wholly** is derived from the word "whole", meaning entirely, in full, throughout. Used in conjunction with the word **other,** it becomes a category in which the two distinct entities of the sacred and profane interactivate and transcend one another.

The dynamic aspect of the **wholly other** reveals its infinite nature. Its scope is to transcend all cultural and religious boundaries into the **all inclusive.**

The wholly other stems from the antagonism of the sacred and profane reality. It transcends the sacred's own **exclusivity** by opening up to the profane into the all inclusive dynamic truth. As we saw, Job lived through both realities: the sacred and the profane. Hence, the wholly other transcends one state of religious reality into another. In other words, it is Job's transition from the sacred to the profane reality that underlines the fundamental essence of the wholly other.

It is his experience of being both included and excluded from the sacred that allows Job to **see** the **whole** reality of God: the sacred and the profane.

Surprisingly, it is through the profane that Job has a glimpse of the whole and **other** nature of the divine reality. Step by step, as he moves away from the sacred into the profane, he experiences the all **inclusive.** His apperception of the whole becomes in effect a revelation of God.

the wholly other

sacred   vs   profane

•

The prologue describes a special relationship between God and Job. Similar to Genesis, it is disturbed by the arrival of an **alien:** the serpent in Genesis, and Satan in Job. As the account reveals, Job is abandoned by God for the sake of the **adversary.** The special relationship between God and his servant is broken. By the same token an order is broken and Job is precipitated into the unknown.

At the end of the narrative Job is reinstated into God's favor. God restores everything Job had lost and much more. Job doubles his wealth. Family and friends return. He has many other children.

As Job's innocence is vindicated, he nevertheless submits to the theological premise that God transcends any human prerogative, as he confesses:

> I had **heard** of thee by the hearing of the ear,
> but now my eye **sees** thee
> Therefore I despise myself, and repent
> in dust and ashes.

In a final remorseful outburst, he recognizes his own mortality and bows to God's immortality. He yields to God's eternal prerogative.

•

To conclude, our hero was excluded from God and community, while Yahweh and Israel excluded themselves from the outside world. The first is a profane experience, the second is sacred. The profane experience of Job is related to a predominant patriarchal order. Because he belonged to that order, he only temporarily sojourns into the realm of the profane. Time enough to see God, and only to reemerge with greater glory. In keeping with this reasoning, the profane reality of the Goddess, as depicted in the metaphors of Genesis and Exodus, is indefinitely kept overshadowed by the overpowering patriarchal order of the God of the Fathers.

PART TWO

NEW TESTAMENT TRADITION: The Holy Trinity

Savoir n'est rien, imaginer est tout.

Anatole France
"Le Crime de Sylvestre Bonnard"

GOD THE FATHER: The Patriarchal Tradition

We ended the first part of the book with the definition of three principles: the sacred, the profane, and the wholly other. In the next five chapters we will describe the spiritual reality of the Father, the Son, and the Holy Spirit in the Trinity and portray an analogy between the two triads. To do so, we will develop each "person" of the Trinity according to its specific identity and function. We will also disclose the relevance and **exclusion** of the Mother of God in the sacred triad.

But since the oldest biblical divinity is that of God of the Fathers, we will start our analogy with the patriarchal figure.

El, Elohim

One of the oldest Semitic appellatives of God is *'el*.[1] The designation has been widely used in ancient Israel, Babylonia, and Arabia. It is also found in the oldest names as a component of: Ishma-*el*, Bethu-*el*, and Isra-*el*.[2] The original meaning of the word *'el* is still uncertain, but a probable origin may stem from the root *'lh*, which conveys the sense of "to be strong and powerful", "direction", or

---

[1] The term Semitic is used here to represent the family of languages of which Hebrew, Aramaic, Ethiopic and ancient Assyrian are a part.

[2] *Ilumma-ila* and *Ibni-ilu,* in Babylonia; *IlL-awwas* and *Jasma'-ilu* in Southern Arabia.

even "a sphere of control". We also find the root alongside the proper name of deities such as: El-Shaddai (God Almighty), El-Elyon (God Most High), and El-Roi ("El sees me", "God Seeing").[3]

Among the most appropriate epithets of El are "Mighty", "Leader", or "Governor". Its most forceful significance was meant to stress an attribute of majesty, with the intent to inspire fear in the face of God's "mighty" presence. Another important feature in the Scriptures is the frequent use of the appellative El in connection with the patriarchs' names. The "God of Abraham" for instance, is the "El of Abraham", the "Fear of Isaac" is the "El of Isaac", and the "Mighty One of Jacob" is the "El of Jacob". The designation was also used to describe the "God of the fathers"; ie, the "El of the Fathers".[4] This feature indicates a special relation between the deity and the individual leader. The God of the leader became, henceforth, the God of the family and of the tribe. As such it also established a tribal **bond** between *the* God and the group.

> Gen. 33:18 And Jacob came safely to the city of Shechem, which is the land of Canaan, on his way from Paddanaram; and he camped before the city. And from the sons of Hamor, Shechem's father, he bought for a hundred pieces of money the piece of land on which he had pitched his tent. There he erected an altar and called it **El-Elo'he-Israel** (that is God, the God of Israel).

•

Several divinities of the ancient near East in the second millennium BC were, for the most part, assigned to a specific cultic place. The more stable kingdoms living during that period were constantly threatened by wandering nomadic tribes. War was an ongoing reality, especially among the emerging powers seeking to expand their dominion. The survival of the smaller semi-nomadic tribes depended on the initiative of their leader.

The pervasive use of "magic" in connection to their tribal "gods" was common as a way to inspire confidence, strength, and protection against rival enemies. The religious life of the group was closely intertwined into the nuclear social structure. Herdsmen, clans, and tribes, most of them semi-nomadic, were constantly in search of new ways to provide for their own subsistence and that of their flock in a harsh environment. The best fertile lands were

---

[3] El-Shaddai (Gen. 17:1); El-Elyon (Gen. 14:18f); and El-Roi (Gen. 22:14).

[4] El of Abraham (Gen. 31:53); El of Isaac (Gen. 31:42); El of Jacob (Gen. 49:24).

72

already occupied by the powerful rulers of the city-states.[5]

The text of Genesis reveals that the worship of El among the early Hebrew migrant tribes had the same specific function of social cohesion and protection. Consequently, the random contact with other tribes and cultures brought about spontaneous opposition to rival cultic deities which endangered the integrity and cohesion of the group. This is especially the case of El and its opposition to Baal, the warrior storm-god, the King of the Gods.[6]

•

Another word commonly used for God in the Old Testament is *'elohim*.[7] Etymologically it is connected to El. It is used mostly as an "abstract plural" or a "plural of intensity". Elohim can best be translated into the Godhead. It is mostly used as a superlative to elevate the rank of the divinity above the pantheon of the other gods. This expression was utilized primarily in Babylonia and in pre-Israelite Palestine to express the unity of individual gods that combined the totality of the higher divine reality. The plural form became recognized as an expression of superiority. In that sense, the narrative uses the plural form of *'elohim* to glorify the God of Sinai as the supreme divinity, and to express the superiority of God—*'elohim*—to other gods.

The name Elohim is also a generic term for God which is used to replace the name Yahweh. Among other epithets used in the Bible to replace the unspeakable name of God—YHWH—is Adonai, or the LORD.

Yahweh

El, in all likelihood, is linked etymologically to *ilu,* a widely popular high-god of ancient Mesopotamia and the most prominent deity in the Canaanite religion. El, which we have identified with the God worshipped by the fathers, was also a prevalent God in Canaan, what was commonly known as Palestine.[8]

---

[5] See Max Weber, Ancient Judaism, New York, The Free Press, 1952.

[6] See M. Weber, Ibid., 154. Also Walther Eichrodt, Theology of the Old Testament, London, SCM Press, 1969, 180, Gerhard von Rad, Old Testament Theology, London, Oliver and Boyd, 1965, and Edmond Jacob, Old Testament Theology, New York, Harper and Brothers, 1955, 56.

[7] Gen. 1:26; 20:13; etc.

[8] Ronald E. Clements, The God of Israel, Atlanta, John Knox Press, 1979, 64.

Ex. 6:2 And God said to Moses, "I am the LORD. I appeared to Abraham, to Isaac, and to Jacob, as God Almighty, but by my name the LORD I did not make myself known to them. I also established my covenant with them, to give them the land of Canaan, the land in which they dwelt as sojourners."

P, who wrote the quote above, makes it quite clear that the identity of the gods worshipped by the forefathers are not to be mistaken with Yahweh, who disclosed himself to Moses for the first time. In the text, Yahweh informs Moses that he was known by the forefathers as El Shaddai; ie, the God Almighty. The account also reveals the whole **new** reality of Yahweh who links the promise he made to Abraham, Isaac, and Jacob, and finally to Moses.

Yahweh's promise links his presence to the enduring existence of his people's posterity; ie, the descendants and the race. A promise which is revived again and again through the kings and prophets in whom Yahweh chooses to inspire his authority.

Ex. 3:14 God said to Moses, "I AM WHO I AM". And he said, "Say this to the people of Israel, 'I AM has sent me to you.' "

In the quote above J links God's name with the verb "to be", or "to exist".

Ehyeh-asher-ehyeh[9]
I AM WHO I AM

The significance of the tautology *ehyeh-asher-ehyeh,* with the emphasis on the redundancy of the verb *ehyeh,* "to be", is meant to enforce the idea of vitality and presence. The context in which God speaks, and to whom he speaks, implies an apperception of the divine presence which is linked with the promise made by God to the forefathers.[10]

The essence of the being of God is portrayed in terms of presence and of relationship. All the attributes are closely related to the twofold relationship between Yahweh and Moses and the realization

---

[9] Torah, Philadelphia, The Jewish Publication Society of America, 1982, Ex. 3:14.

[10] One interesting hypothesis on the origin of YHWH—called the tetragrammaton—relates to an extension of the prehistoric word *hu* rendered "He", the god. Another similarity points to the Dervish cry *Ya-hu* which can be translated into "O He". The original expression may have been *Ya-huva,* if the Arabic pronoun *huwa* is taken to mean "he". It is possible that the name *Ya-huva* could have meant "O-He" also. Such an expression could easily have evolved into *Yahu* and finally *Yahweh.* It is also interesting to note the rhetorical character in the original use of the word. M. Buber, Moses, Oxford, Phaidon Press Ltd, 49f.

of the promise to free the people from Egypt.[11] The closeness is explained when God says to Moses, "But I will be with you".[12]

When God tells Moses to go to the people and tell them that "I AM has sent me to you", he implies that when the hero utters the words "I AM", Moses will assume and ultimately embody God's divine authority. Yahweh's personal presence and existence is, shall we say, determined by Moses' acquiescence of his mission. Yet it is the ongoing quality of the promise that is eternal, not God's spokesmen. As such, the promise transcends Moses' historicity.

Individuality is also stressed by the pronoun "I" which can only exist in the act of speaking to others or to oneself.[13] Yet the first person singular indicates the presence of the imageless *individuum vaguum*. In the narrative the "I" exists—or stands out—as an individual being since God's words are audible and comprehensible to the hero even though God's reality is imageless. As God introduces himself, a distance is set between Yahweh and Moses. The alienation stems from the mystery of the distant promise that God had made to the forefathers. But as soon as Moses realizes the scope of his destiny, the hero finally understands the message and goal of the revelation. Then, the separation narrows. As Moses accepts God's mission, he eventually identifies with the promise. More so when Yahweh reassures Moses that he will be with him and that his mouth will be God's mouth. At the outset Yahweh is **wholly other** than Moses, yet he becomes **one** with him in his mission.

•

Although God forbids the use of any "graven images" to portray or to identify him, the text is full of metaphors to suggest that his identity is accessible to us:

Ex. 33:11 "Thus the LORD used to speak to Moses face to face, as a man speaks to his friend".

God here is depicted as a friend, and the intimacy of the relationship is further symbolized by its anthropomorphical and metaphorical nature.

Throughout the Bible, the narrative uses the anthropomorphical to reveal God.

---

[11] See Martin Buber, Moses, Oxford, Phaidon Press Ltd, 192-195.

[12] Ex. 3:12.

[13] See Ivan Illich and Barry Sanders', ABC: The Alphabetization of the Popular Mind, San Francisco, North Point Press, 1988, 70f.

Gen.	1:3	> God speaks
Gen.	1:26	> God created man in his image
Gen.	3:8	> God walks in the garden
Gen.	32.24	> God wrestles with Jacob
Exod.	15:8	> God has a nose
Deut.	11:12	> God has eyes
1 Sam.	8:21	> God has ears
Ps.	2:4	> God laughs
Isa.	42:14	> God pants and groans

We have seen in Genesis how God **speaks** to the world. He speaks to his prophets, to his people, and to the reader. This ability to **communicate** is essential in order for his will to be known.

God was present in the beginning. He was present with Abraham, Jacob, Isaac, and Moses. God is always present in his **promise.** Therefore, God transcends the personal relationship to encompass the **people** and their **progeny** in order that the promise be safeguarded.

the historical . . . Yahweh is the God of the Patriarchs, of Moses, of the anointed Kings, of the Prophets, and the priests etc. . .

---

the eternal . . . . . God's promise to his people from which he chooses his spokesman

•

The main purpose of this chapter was to put in proper perspective the specific identity of the God of the Old Testament. As we have seen, God, in ancient Judaism, evolved from a more general Semitic designation of El into the more exclusive appellation of YHWH (Yahweh). All the divine designations used in the Bible are but pseudonyms of Yahweh. Therefore, only the **unspeakable YHWH** is the holy one, and only he is the center of worship. A God vehemently opposed to any other god(s). He is the **exclusive** and **ineffable** religious reality of Israel.

GOD THE SON: The Scapegoat

A logical sequence to the previous chapter brings us to the person of Jesus Christ although the concept of the Incarnation is not present in the Old Testament since any image of God is forbidden. As we have said, in Judaism the name of Yahweh is so sacred that it is not even uttered. And even though the Old and the New Testaments appear incompatible in view of this conflicting and fundamental issue, the Gospels advocate and describe a transition between the old tradition and a new one. The New Testament inaugurates another religious reality: that of the Son of God, the Word Incarnate.

The word Gospel is a derivative of *godspel,* meaning "good tidings". The original word in Greek meant "the good news" translated from the Hebrew word *bissar,* meaning "herald of good tidings" or "to bring the good news of salvation".[1]

None of the authors of the Gospels knew or met Jesus. Their personal account of the life of Jesus is nonetheless a revelation of their own **faith** in Christ. Unlike the Pentateuch each Gospel is written by a single author. They were in all likelihood written between 70 and 90 AD.

The core of the narratives that relates the life of Jesus is made up of the three synoptic Gospels. These accounts are called synoptic because they share a common perspective; they are the Gospels of

---

[1] Isa. 40:9; 52:7; 61:1, etc.

Matthew, Mark, and Luke. The fourth one, the Gospel of John, does not share the same chronology of Jesus' life.[2] Matthew and Luke have a richer material than Mark, and although they complement each other, they also differ in many important facts.

We will not debate here the synoptic problem of the parallels and incongruities between the texts. Instead we will focus on the fundamental themes and chronology of Jesus' life.

In accordance with tradition, the Gospel of Matthew begins with the **genealogy** of Joseph, Jesus' legal father. This most important theme of the Bible is carefully perpetuated in the first narrative. From Adam, to "the generations of Adam", to Noah, to Shem, and to Abraham, etc. . .[3] The evangelist establishes Joseph as the legal heir to the Fathers. Notwithstanding that Jesus is not Joseph's biological son but his legal one.

Among the ancestors enumerated in the genealogy are the names of four women: Tamar, Rahab, Ruth, and Bathshebah (Uriah's wife). One explanation for their presence in a patriarchal lineage is perhaps to make a connection between Mary's unusual "virginal" conception and the irregular nature of the union of these women with their own partners.[4] For instance, Tamar took the initiative in her scandalous union with Judah. Rahab had been a prostitute but she nevertheless made it possible for Israel to enter the promised land. Ruth was responsible for an irregular union with Boaz without which there may not have been a Davidic line. And finally Uriah's wife, Bethshebah, had an affair with David that resulted in the birth of Solomon.

In post-biblical Jewish piety, the circumstances surrounding these unconventional events were seen as the work of the Spirit of God. All these examples show the unfathomable and intriguing nature of God's intervention in human affairs as a way to influence the course of history.

•

In Matthew, the dreams of Joseph are paralleled with Joseph (in Genesis) whose ability to read dreams brought his people into Egypt and saved them from famine. Joseph, in the New Testament, also has dreams where God tells him to flee to Egypt in order to save Jesus from the murderous hands of Herod. By bringing Jesus

---

[2] Paul Feine, Johannes Behm, and reedited by Werner Georg Kummel, Introduction to the New Testament, New York, Abington Press, 1966.

[3] Mt. 1:1-16; Gen. 5:1-31; 10:1-32; 11:10-31.

[4] The second explanation, made popular by Luther, interprets the inclusion of these four women as the symbolic presence of foreigners—Gentiles or persons associated with Gentiles in Bethshibah's case—in God's plan.

to **Egypt** he providentially relives the experience of the people of Israel.[5]

Biblical typology

Old Testament sequence:

Joseph's dreams bring his people to Egypt and save them from famine.

Moses escapes from the wicked hands of the Pharaoh.

Moses delivers his people out of Egypt to the promised land.

Moses wanders forty years in the desert.

New Testament sequence:

Joseph's dreams bring his family to Egypt and save his child from Herod.

Jesus escapes from the hands of the wicked Herod

Joseph leaves Egypt and comes back to Galilee

Jesus fasts forty days in the desert

As soon as the Pharaoh dies, Moses is able to return safely to Egypt. Likewise, Jesus is able to return to Nazareth as soon as Herod dies. Upon Jesus' return from Egypt, he relives the Exodus and the coming to the promised land.

Moses' untimely death unables him to see the promised land and the journey is completed by **Joshua.** The name **Jesus** is a nickname of Joshua. The analogy and symbolism underlined by the typologies are insightful.

The Evangelists describe the link between the Old tradition and the New. Moses didn't live to see the promised land, Joshua did. Therefore, when the Virgin Mary is told to call her son Jesus— Joshua—a new quest for the promised land has begun.

In the beginning of his journey Jesus is first led away from Bethlehem, the city of David, the King of Jews, and brought back to Galilee, the land of the Gentiles. He takes up residence in Nazareth where he begins his mission and becomes known as Jesus the Naz-

---

[5] Raymond E. Brown, The Birth of the Messiah, New York, Images Books, 1979.

arean. Here the Gospels have taken up the difficult task of reconciling the Old tradition with the New in announcing the "good news" to all the people, Jews and Gentiles alike.

Yahweh	vs	Father
Moses	vs	Jesus
God of the Fathers	vs	*Abba;* dad
1st commandment	vs	the Son of God
jealous God	vs	loving God
Israel	vs	all the people

Jesus' identity is best related to in terms of his relationship with his God and the world. He described himself as a spiritual physician, a shepherd to his people, a divinely authorized prophet. Foremost, Jesus calls himself the "Son of man". This latter epithet may have been used by Jesus as a way to describe himself simply as "someone" in the quality of "a human being". He also described his God simply as *abba* or "dear father", or **dad.** In this sense the relationship between him and his Father is a very **personal** and intimate one.

•

During Pompey's conquest of Jerusalem in 63 BC, the priests ruled Israel. It was under the control of the Roman emperors Antony and Octavian that the reign of Herod the Great began (37-4 BC). Herod was known to be tyrannical yet competent. He was subservient to Rome but harsh and violent with his people. At his death he divided his kingdom among his three sons. Rome, however, did not confer upon them the title of king. The kingdom of Judaea and the title of ethnarch was bestowed to Archelaus. The kingdom of Galilee and Perea was given to Antipas, also known as Herod the tetrarch whom Jesus called "that fox": the one who executed John the Baptist. And finally, the north-eastern territory of the Sea of Galilee, was given to Philip with the title of tetrarch also. Of all the three sons, Archelaus was most like his father, except that he was more violent and less competent. For that reason, representatives of the Jewish aristocracy went to Rome to complain about the despotic ruler hoping that Rome would allow them to reinstate a Jewish theocracy. Augustus recognized their plea and banished Archelaus from his office but put Judaea under the status of a third-class province governed by a procurator appointed by Rome.

At that time, the territory of Judaea, especially Jerusalem, was the center of Jewish worship. Jerusalem, more precisely its temple, was believed to be the heart of true Judaism. The territory outside it was considered to be unclean and impure. This was particularly the case of neighboring Galilee which was made up of a Jewish and non-Jewish population of Syrians and Greeks, still heavily influenced by Hellenism.[6]

The change in the political status of Judaea also meant that it had to pay its taxes directly to Rome. This enraged a number of Jewish people because it was considered **sacrilegious** to pay tribute directly to a foreign and heathen ruler. To appease the Jews, and as a gesture of good will, Augustus decreed that synagogues were inviolable and Jews were to be exempt from appearing in court on their Sabbath.[7]

It was because of the foreign collection of these taxes that Judas the Galilaean led a Jewish revolt against Rome in 6 AD. Although the uprising was firmly suppressed, the seeds of discontent were rooted among the radicals of the land. Rebellious ideals were further fomented by a group of Zealots that kept the spirit of revolt alive for the next two generations.

The peaceful coexistence between the procurators and the high priests went on more or less smoothly inasmuch as the high priests continued to pay the Roman representatives bribes to keep their office. It was a practice that accommodated the priests and enriched the procurators. It is not surprising that under these circumstances the high-priesthood had lost the respect of the population. Only the richest priestly families were able to retain their sacred office. Such was the case of Joseph Caiaphas (18-36 AD) who managed to keep his office despite the nomination of Poncious Pilate (26-36 AD). These arrangements, however, did not guarantee a good relationship between Rome and Judaea.

It turned out that Poncious Pilate had an uncanny ability to offend Jewish susceptibility. On one occasion, in an act of deliberate spite, he had put a dedication to the Emperor on Herod's palace. The Jewish elite was greatly insulted by it. They soon sent a deputation to Tiberius to complain about the emblem. They argued that the procurator had not put his name on the Jerusalem's palace to honor him but simply to annoy them. Tiberius in a gesture of good will ordered the shields to be taken down.

Although Rome was firmly in control of Judaea, it shared some of its power with the clerical elite as a peaceful accommodation. The Pharisees, the Sadducees, and the Essenes, were among the

---

[6] Emil Schurer, A History of the Jewish People in the Time of Jesus, New York, Schocken Books, 1971.

[7] F.F. Bruce, Israel And The Nations, Grand Rapids, Wm. B. Eerdmans Publishing Co., 1963.

priestly schools of thought—*haeresis*—which began to flourish during the Hasmonean resistance (167-164 BC).

The Pharisees believed in the written laws of Moses, but contrary to the Sadducees and the Essenes, they also believed in the oral laws handed down to them by the Fathers. They believed in the resurrection of the body for the good soul, and eternal damnation for the wicked. The name Pharisees is derived from the Greek translation of the Hebrew *perushim* meaning separatists, deviants, or heretics. They were called so because these people were so scrupulous about the laws and rituals that they separated themselves from the less observant masses, the *'ammei ha-arets*.[8]

The Sadducees were the other major group of priests that flourished in Jerusalem during Jesus's life. They claimed to be the direct descendants of Zadok, the high priest in Solomon's temple. They were called *tseduquim*. Contrary to the Pharisees, they believed that only the written laws were to be observed. This brought the Pharisees and the Sadducees in bitter conflict. In addition, the Sadducees did not share the Pharisees' belief in the immortality of the soul nor did they believe in the resurrection of the body. Despite all their differences they managed to coexist and the two groups shared their priestly duties in the temple. The most notorious Sadducee is Caiaphas, the high priest who took part in Jesus' trial.

The Pharisees had come to formulate a doctrine of the two realms: render unto Caesar what is Caesar's and unto God what is God's. In accordance to this doctrine the Pharisees tolerated that the people paid their taxes to Rome. It permitted a compromise in matters regarding the state, as long as it did not interfere with their religious affairs.

But the compromise was seen by the more radical groups as an act of treason. A group of these revolutionaries, called the Fourth Philosophy, gave the Romans and Jewish collaborators a hard time until they all committed suicide in the fortress of Masada in 73 AD.

Among the many priestly characteristics that are severely criticized by Jesus in the narrative is their scrupulous and hypocritical application of the law. The overwhelming preoccupation with purity and reward supplanted a simple and unadorned piety. The conscientious concern with legal requirements mostly void of any inward religious feelings transformed the ethical into the judicial: the moral and religious were replaced by the legal and formal. In

---

[8] In the New Testament the Pharisees are also identified as the scribes and the sages; Mat. 2:4; 21:15; 23:15. See Ellis Rivkin, What Crucified Jesus?, London, SCM Press Ltd, 1986.

other words, the Spirit of the law was replaced by the letter of the law and by endless litigation.

Pharisees/scribes

sacred/law	vs	profane/common
pietists	vs	masses
pure	vs	impure
clean	vs	unclean

Every single aspect of the historical, political, economical, social, and religious context in which Jesus Christ lived and died is important. Every one of these factors help to understand the development of events that led to the culmination of Jesus Christ.

As we will see, the miracles are the clearest **signs** of Jesus' earthly activity. They delineate whom Jesus privileged with his **presence.** The miracles are the signs that separate those who were metamorphosed by his message and those who opposed it. Among his opponents were the priests and the religious elite of Jerusalem.

The Gospels recount Jesus' mission among the people, who for the most part were outcasts. The narratives show that he directed the attention on them by performing his miracles. The narratives describe these miracles as **signs.**[9] The narratives also use the words "mighty deeds", and "manifestations of power". The term power here should be understood in the sense of Jesus' active **presence** among the outcasts who have no rank or standing among the "principalities and powers" of this world. The miracles are meant to point out the **significant** social condition in which the outcasts live. In this context the miracles are a **banner** that circumscribe Jesus' ministry.

In the Old Testament the **sign** is used as the invisible active power of God. The book of Genesis shows how numerous symbols of nature are used to emphasize the sacred events in history. Similarly, in Genesis the sun and the moon are signs—symbols—for seasons, days and years, the circumcision, "a sign of the covenant" (Gen. 17:10), and the sign of blood on the door in Exodus heralds the "pass over" (Ex. 12:13). God uses signs as symbols to indicate his will to the "hearer".

---

[9] J.T. Maertens, La Structure des Récits de Miracles dans les Synoptiques, in, Sciences Religieuses/Religious Studies, 6/3, (1976-77), 253-266.

Isa. 7:13 And he said, "Hear then, O house of David! Is it too little for you to weary men, that you weary my God also? Therefore the LORD himself will give you a **sign.** Behold, a young woman (or virgin) shall conceive and bear a son and shall call his name Imman'u-el."[10]

•

The first miracle related in the Gospels of Matthew and Luke is the virginal conception. The quote of Isaiah above is an important parallel that links the virginal birth of Jesus to the Old Testament. Throughout the narratives the Evangelists take a great deal of care in legitimizing Jesus as the Messiah prophesied in the Bible. The reason for such a concern becomes clearer as Jesus is confronted by accusations from the religious elite about his origins and authority. Not only does Jesus come from Galilee, the land of the aliens and heathens, but he arrogantly questions the honesty of the priesthood. They, in return, challenge the origin of his power to perform miracles since only God can perform miracles.[11]

We have talked about the miracles as signs that circumscribe Jesus' message of faith. The physical account of the cures, the exorcisms, the raising of the dead, the multiplication of the breads, all point to a violation of the laws of nature. Since all four Evangelists, each in their own way, confirm the reality of the physical aspect of the miracles in the narrative, it is impossible to fully elucidate their reality. Although the mystery involving their physical nature and origin may not be explained, these "signs" point to the whole purpose of Jesus' ministry rather than the mysterious origin of his powers. In this sense, he uses the miracles to direct the attention toward a certain category of people, who for the most part, are segregated by society. His aim is to circumscribe the alien and marginal side of the religious reality.

types of miracles

1) the healings: sick, lepers, handicapped
2) exorcisms: casting out demon and evil spirits
3) feeding the hungry and poor
4) raising the dead
5) calming the storm, changing the water into wine

---

[10] The young woman can also be rendered into "virgin".

[11] Deut. 13:1-11.

who benefits from the miracles

1) the forgotten: the sick, the poor, and the hungry
2) the outcasts: the lepers, the possessed
3) the helpless: the handicapped, the dead
4) the foreigners: Romans, strangers, pagans
5) the outsiders: the women, the children

If we take a close look at the list above, we can illustrate the beneficiaries as the **powerless**: the ignored and the forgotten of society.

On the opposite side, those who reject the miracles and condemn Jesus:

Jesus' adversaries

1) the Pharisees, the scribes, the Sadducees, the high priest Caiaphas
2) the elders, the lawyers (Lk. 11:52)
3) the crowds, and the cities (Mt. 8:34, 11:20-24)
4) the merchants in the temple
5) the Roman procurator

This list characterizes the **powerful.** If we look into this classification more closely, we can detect the whole spectrum of power and hierarchy in society:

the spiritual: the high priest, Sadducees, the Pharisees

the intellectual: the Pharisees, the scribes, the lawyers

the economical: the high priest, the merchants

the political: the Roman procurator, the high priest, the crowd, the Zealots.

Hence the antagonism appears as follows:

the *powerful*   vs   the *powerless*

•

From the beginning, Jesus' religious authority is questioned by the skeptics, setting "apart" those who believe and those who reject Jesus Christ. Drawing the boundaries of his Kingdom of God, Jesus' realm is set up against the worldly powers. The antagonism becomes even more evident as it culminates with his crucifixion. The progression of events that leads to Jesus' death unfolds quickly. On the cross, except for a few loyal followers, he is abandoned by all, even God.

As the drama unfolds, Jesus gathers numerous followers. At the same time he is confronted by an increasing number of foes. The dividing line between them becomes clearer. His message of love widens the gap between those who believe him and those who reject him. With the Sermon on the Mount, Jesus inaugurates a new law in which love is the only requisite. This new law transcends the old one, which further antagonizes the religious elite of Jerusalem.[12]

Although the Evangelists take great care in legitimizing Jesus as the Messiah, the priests of Jerusalem question his authority because of his Galilean origin. From the outset Jesus is opposed by the religious authority of the priests and scribes. They are offended by Jesus' interpretation of the law. Furthermore, he performs miracles freely on the Sabbath, breaking the law. To that effect he answers them: "The Sabbath was made for man, not man for the Sabbath . . .".[13]

But the priests also object to him because the Old Testament warns that only God can perform miracles. Hence, if a prophet performs "signs and wonders" he shall be put to death because the LORD is testing the people to see if they are faithful to him.[14]

But a greater blasphemy than ignoring the Sabbath is the identity of Jesus himself. He declares himself the Son of God, "I and the Father are one".[15] Not only does Jesus challenge the first commandment of an imageless God but he declares himself to be that God. This is how he justifies his identity:

> Jn. 8:58 Jesus said to them, "Truly, truly, I say to you, before Abraham was, **I am.**"
>
> 10:34 "Is it not written in your law, 'I said, you are gods'?"

Because of this, they want to stone him. Just like they wanted to stone the adulteress that Jesus saved from their hands. They also accuse him of being a "demon" and a "Samaritan". In other words, they associate him with the outcasts, women/prostitutes, the foreigners, and the possessed.

---

[12] Mt. 5:1-48; Lk. 6:20-49.

[13] Mk. 2:27

[14] Deut. 13:1-13.

[15] Jn. 10:30.

Jesus is accused of being:

blasphemous
possessed by a demon
a Samaritan, a Nazareen, a foreigner

The blasphemies seem to confirm the religious elite's fears about Jesus. It also justifies their schemes to plot his death. Slowly, behind the scenes, a mischievous consensus is fomenting against him. Like Job, Jesus becomes the target of the political and religious authorities.

Mk. 3:6 The Pharisees went out, and immediately held counsel with the Hero'di-ans against him, how to destroy him.[16]

•

He is not only rejected by the elite but by society as a whole.

During his passage in Gadarenes, Jesus is met by two wild demoniacs who ask him to cast their devils out and send them away among the herd of swine that could be seen close by. Jesus complies. As soon as he does, the whole herd is taken by a frenzy and jumps from a cliff into the sea to perish in the water below. With great consternation the herdsmen go to the city to report the event they just witnessed.

Mt. 8:34 And behold, **all** the **city** came out to meet Jesus; and when they saw him, they begged him to leave their neighborhood.

Not surprised by this Christ warns his disciple about society and hierarchy.

Jn. 15:18 If the world hates you, know that it has hated me before it hated you. **If you were of the world, the world would love its own; but because you are not of the world, but I chose you out of the world, therefore the world hates you.**

Did the **crowd** chase him away because he destroyed the herd, threatening their livelihood? Apparently, the city was not ready to pay the price with their livelihood to save two poor demoniacs.

Even Jerusalem, of all cities, is typified as an example:

---

[16] The Herodians were political functionaries influential in the court of Herod Antipas.

Mt. 23:37 "O Jerusalem, Jerusalem, killing the prophets and stoning those who are sent to you!"

Several other cities like Nazareth are mentioned by Jesus as being blind to his message:

Mk. 6:4 "A prophet is not without honour, except in his own country, and among his own kin, and in his own house."

He goes even further by saying that he has seen more faith in a Roman centurion than in anybody else in Israel.[17]

But this, it seems, is only a prelude to what is going to happen later when the whole vengeful crowd in Jerusalem rallies against him and demands his death. The collectivity is seen as having a **power** of its own, obeying its own laws of inertia. As it turns out, the **mob** gathered at his trial will be Jesus' final and fatal foe.

•

The word "messiah" means the anointed one or the one who is consecrated by anointing for a special function among the people of God. It originally was used to describe the consecration of a king. This ritual was widespread among the cultures of the ancient Near East.[18] In Judaism this function is typified by Samuel's anointing of Saul and later of David as the king of Judah and Israel. Kingship occupied an important place in the theology of Israel. The Davidic era is the golden age of Israel. It is the time when Israel lived at the epitome of its political and religious integrity; when it had complete control over its destiny.

The peace and prosperity of the kingdom of David came to an end with the Assyrian wars (745-721 BC). The loss of the golden era inspired among its people a longing for another Messiah. They sought for redeemer, an heir of David, who would bring an end to the misery of foreign conquest. It would enable the people to return from their exile.[19]

At the root of **messianism** is the religious and political quest for liberation. In times of great despair, the messianic expectations increase. Messianism became the expression of spiritual consolation for a paradise lost and the hope for the return of past glory.

---

[17] Mt. 8:10.

[18] In Is. 45:1, the Persian king Cyrus is addressed by Yahweh as "his anointed". See also; Jg. 9:8,15; 1 Sam. 10:1, 2 Sam. 2:4; 5:3.

[19] Is. 9:1-6; 2 Sam. 7:16; Is. 55:3-5.

The pursuit of freedom from foreign influence is at the root of the messianic promise of salvation. Results of recent ethnological studies show that various forms of messianism evolve from a disastrous repercussion of foreign domination and colonialism. The ambiguous feelings of seduction and revulsion toward foreign culture is always coupled by a radical polarization. It imprints ambivalent feelings of **lord-victim.**

The crisis, propelled by the presence of a foreign culture, threatens the structure of belief from without. Messianism is linked to a perceived threat to the indigenous culture. A fear of loss of religious integrity and collective identity. As a result, the movement revives hopes of messianic salvation that rekindle an idealized past. It instigates a return to these original ideals in their purest form in order to bolster a strong sense of identity. The anxiety provoked by acculturation encourages the radical belief of messianic redemption, often by revolutionary means, which triggers a radical antagonism to the domination of foreign cultures. The rebellion is usually instigated by the elite who perceive the threat as an immediate danger to their own survival. Messianic movements typically nourish mythical expressions of hope. They revert to powerful images of salvation that capture the "spirit" of the people. The threat of assimilation by the people is then perceived as a personal threat to their own identity and survival.[20]

The circumstances under which Christ—the Greek equivalent for the word messiah—makes his appearance in Jerusalem are singular. The narratives describe that Jesus accepts the triumphant procession in Jerusalem riding on a donkey like the "son of David" on Palm Sunday. As we know, his role is not a political one, but that of a spiritual Messiah announcing a kingdom that is not of this world.[21]

•

Throughout the Gospels Jesus is determined not to be manipulated by any group. He stands firm on his own unique identity. He refuses to comply to the rules set by the priests. He declines to take up the cause of the nationalist Zealots. As he said, his mission is not of this world. He rejects Satan's offer to indulge in the riches

---

[20] The Islamic Revolution in Iran is a case in point. Here are some additional references on messianism: W. Muhlmann, Messianismes Révolutionnaires du Tiers-Monde, Paris, Gallimard, 1968; G. Devereux, Ethnopsychanalyse Complémentariste, Paris, Flamarion, 1972, and by the same author, Essais D'Ethnopsychiatrie Générale, Paris, Gallimard, 1970; also the interesting book by, F. Laplantine, L'Ethnopsychiatrie, Paris, Editions Universitaires, Paris, 1973, and his other work, Les Trois Voix de l'Imaginaire, Paris, Editions Universitaires, 1974.

[21] Mk. 14:61-65; Dan. 7:13.

of the world. And he spurns the idea to exploit his powerful charisma for his personal economic or political gain. He stands firm on his grounds. He declares himself to be the Son of man and the Son of God.

He applies the same determination to his fate. He knows about his oncoming death. But he will not try to change the course of destiny, though he could at any time.

At his arrest, one after the other, his disciples abandon him to his captors. Apparently, they thought Jesus to be someone else:

> Lk. 24:21 . . . we had hoped that he was the one to redeem Israel.

When Jesus is betrayed by Judas, he is brought in front of the Sanhedrin where he is finally confronted by his **adversaries.**[22]

Caiaphas, the Sadducean high priest, is present among the crowd of Pharisees and scribes who have already decided on Jesus' death. But they have a problem: they must find a way to inculpate him. At his interrogation, Jesus is questioned about his identity. He is asked if he is the Son of God, he replies that he is. He also answers them that he is the Son of man who will be at the right hand of the **Power.**

Upon his reply, they accuse him of blasphemy and condemn him to death. Shortly after, Jesus is sent to the procurator Pilate, in whose hands rests the political and legal authority over these matters. He states to Jesus that he is being accused by the religious elite of fomenting a revolt against Rome by telling the people not to pay their taxes. He is also accused of proclaiming himself Christ, a king. To his questions Jesus replies:

> Jn. 18:36 "My kingship is not of this world; if my kingship were of this world, my servants would fight, that I might not be handed over to the Jews; but my kingship is not from the world." Pilate said to him, "So you are a king?" Jesus answered, "You say that I am a king. For this I was born, and for this I have come into the world, to bear witness to the truth. Every one who is of the truth hears my voice." Pilate said to him, "What is truth?"

Seeing nothing wrong with Jesus, Pilate turns to the **crowd**

---

[22] There is a parallel here between Judas his disciple and the historical Judas the Galilean, the notorious nationalist.

and he asks them if they want to release Jesus, since it is a custom to free a prisoner during the Passover. Yet the mob demands that Barabbas, a known thief and probably a revolutionary, be released instead.

Here the parallel between Christ's judgement and the sacrificial ritual in Leviticus 16 is compelling. The Old Testament text describes the directives for the Mosaic ritual of the Day of Atonement; to take among the flocks belonging to the people, two male goats. One to be chosen to be sacrificed as a sin-offering to Yahweh, the other as an atonement for Israel's sins and to be set free in the wilderness as an offering to Azazel, the sins of the people having been symbolically laid upon it. Azazel is the name given to a being who opposes Yahweh. The Vulgate version of the Bible rendered the word Azazel into *caper emissarius*.[23] Later, Luther translated the word into *lediger bock* meaning literally free-goat. Finally, the word was rendered into English as **scapegoat:** a victim who is innocently blamed or punished for the sins of others.[24]

The parallel suggests that Jesus is depicted as a human offering to Yahweh. While Barabbas—the name means "son of the father"—who is symbolized as carrying the sins of Israel, is set free to the foreign lands.

The **crowds** that chased him away are now gathered in Jerusalem to demand his death. They choose Barabbas rather than Christ. Jesus who promises the kingdom of God to the **powerless** is a danger to the established order of society. And Caiaphas, as its spokesman, explains why Christ should die:

> Jn. 11:50 "You know nothing at all; you do not understand that it is expedient for you that one man should die for the people, and that the whole nation should not perish."

It is better to sacrifice one person for the sake of the whole society. They perpetuate the false belief that a scapegoat will solve all their problems. Jesus becomes a *pharmakos,* the individual kept by the Greek community as a scapegoat to sacrifice in times of social crisis. But history shows that violence begets violence. The words spoken by Caiaphas are empty words since the temple and Jerusalem will finally be destroyed in 70 AD anyhow. Yet another reason why they seek his death stems from the power of his **word.** They

---

[23] René Girard, The Scapegoat, Baltimore, The Johns Hopkins University Press, 1986.

[24] The Tindale Oxford Dictionary.

think he is fomenting political and religious upheaval. They fear he is seeking to abrogate their power.

But Jesus' prophetic words echo an ultimate truth when he adds:

> Lk. 23:34 "Father, forgive them; for they know not what they do."

Jesus' crucifixion underlines the illusion of violence. Sacrifice and love are the only ways for human salvation.[25]

Although Jesus may be innocent of the crimes he is accused of, he is certainly not a victim. He freely agrees to his fate. He knows and understands the full extent of his decision. His consent is a crucial act of free will. He like Job, as an **individual,** is left alone against all the prejudice and powers of this world. He knows that the powers invested in the political, the social, the economical, and the religious, are present like a dark cloud over him. Jesus knows he has to endure his death so that his absence could be effective. So that his meaningful presence on earth may be resurrected by faith. Only then, can he be of benefit to all. Consequently, he tells his apostles that he must leave in order for his message to be fully understood:

> Jn. 16:7 Nevertheless I tell you the truth: it is to your advantage that I go away.

Only then will they understand that **he** is the message of hope for the **powerless** as the beneficiaries of his kingdom, and not those who already control the **powers** in their own world.

> Mt. 22:16 "Teacher, we know that you are true, and teach the way of God truthfully, and care for no man; for you do not regard the position of men."

They know that the **power** of the word of God is stronger than any human institution. But Jesus clearly did not entice political and economical upheaval. He took great care to share the urgency of the message of love. He introduced a new law to replace the old. He inaugurated a kingdom where women, children, the poor, the

---

[25] "In future, all violence will reveal what Christ's Passion revealed, the foolish genesis of bloodstained idols and the false gods of religion, politics, and ideologies. The murderers remain convinced of the worthiness of their sacrifices. They, too, know not what they do and we must forgive them. The time has come for us to forgive one another. If we wait any longer there will not be time enough". In René Girard's, The Scapegoat, Baltimore, The Johns Hopkins University Press, 1986, 212.

sick, the outcasts, the handicapped, the estranged, the mentally disturbed, the alien, the stranger, and the slave, all have equal access to his kingdom.

•

Jesus Christ's death might appear as an obstacle to his ongoing mission. A timely and tragic obstruction. Far from the truth. His death is precursory to an even greater medium for his message. While on earth he communicated the word of God to the people around him, after his death Jesus embodies a new role in his resurrected body. The risen Christ becomes the ultimate and eternal medium for his message, a personal image to which all have access.

Doctrines about death and resurrection have evolved and changed in the Old Testament. According to the Bible, "man" is not a being composed of a body and a soul but of a soul with the vitality of the flesh. There is no duality between body and soul. "Man" becomes a soul when he is born, and when he dies he is a dead soul. His soul comes directly from God.[26] The word soul in Hebrew means literally a living being, an animated body. Consequently, the dead in Sheol are not the soul of the dead but **shadows** of beings. Accordingly, they are considered **powerless** and **weak**.[27] They could not come back to life.

Job 7:9 . . . he who goes down to Sheol does not come up;

Eccles. 3:19 For the fate of the sons of men and the fate of beasts is the same; as one dies, so dies the other.

The concept evolved and became closely associated with the idea of the restoration of Israel. Particularly in times of historical distress. In Ezechiel, the resurrection of the "dead bones" did not imply a return from Sheol, but a return of the nation from the "dead condition" of exile.[28]

Further development of the concept occurred during the period of the Maccabeans where the belief in the resurrection is clearly expressed:

Dan. 12:2 And many of those who sleep in the dust of the earth shall awake, some to everlasting life, and some to shame and everlasting contempt.

---

[26] Gen. 2:7; Num. 23:10.

[27] Isa. 14:9-11; 26:14; Ps. 88; Job 26:5.

[28] Ezek. 37:1-14.

Later, the chief proponents of the resurrection were the Pharisees. The resurrection was applicable only to a select few like Moses, David, and to the more pious elite of their congregation.

In Christianity, the resurrection of the body became the cornerstone of its faith.

•

The Gospels share basically the same material in respect to the discovery of the empty tomb by a group of women.[29] In all of the accounts, the central figure is a woman called Mary Magdalene. She is Jesus' loved one. She is the **first** person who sees the resurrected body of Christ.

Her name is revealing. Mary was from Magdala—hence Magdalene—a city situated on the west bank of the Sea of Galilee, about 20 km north of Nazareth. The word also means **fortress.**[30]

But what is most peculiar is the time at which she appears in the Gospels. The narrative suddenly acknowledges the presence of this group of women who have been following Jesus during the greater part of his public life but who have been **overshadowed** by the more predominant group of male disciples. Only here, and at a very crucial moment, are the women finally recognized as followers in the same manner as their male counterparts.[31]

If Peter is the metaphorical **rock** on which Jesus built his "Church", then Mary is its **fortress.**

The account also refers to the angels that appear to both male and female apostles. The apparition is also paralleled to the annunciation. Jesus' birth in Mary's **womb** is the counterpart to Mary's presence in front of the empty **tomb.** Birth and death are privileged symbols of life and regeneration. Here, they become kindred to the **resurrection** of Christ.

Christ's death also signifies the sudden emptiness in the followers' lives. The physical absence of their Master leaves them **powerless** and lost. Yet as soon as the news of the empty tomb reaches them, they are filled with hope.

The message from the angels fulfills the prediction about his return:

---

[29] The message is directed to Mary who is described in the narrative as the woman from whom Jesus had cast out seven demons (Lk. 8:2). We can make another parallel with Proverbs 9:13-18 where the **dead** condition and the crazy woman may be linked here with Mary Magdalene.

[30] Jean Daniélou, La Résurrection, Paris, Seuil, 1969, 11.

[31] Lk. 8:2-4; Mk. 15:40-41.

Hos. 6:2 After two days he will **revive** us; on the third day he will raise us up, that we may **live** before him.

Jesus is the bodily proof that God is accessible to us as a person. It is as a person that he was able to establish relationships with his followers. He became the **Word** in order to **communicate** his will directly to the world.

With his resurrected body Jesus becomes the **medium** *par excellence.* His death is no longer an obstacle to his ongoing **message.** With his risen body Christ's message is not limited by the boundaries of time or space. Although his death abruptly ends his physical presence on earth, the heavenly body is eternally present, accessible to all at all times.

the medium

historical	—	*eternal*
Jesus	—	Christ
Judaea	—	all the nations
disciples	—	to all the believers
miracles	—	the resurrection
physical body	—	the resurrected body

Jesus' resurrected body, however, is not the restoration of a previous condition in the flesh, but a transformation of a radical kind. Not to be confused with the decaying nature of the physical body. Christ's resurrection is not a return to a former condition, but the passage to a totally **new** one. With his new condition he is given the title of LORD.

Paul in 1 Corinthians distinguishes the physical body from the spiritual body. The first **is** a body and mortal, the second **has** a body but is spiritual. He also correlates the body to the idea of **image.** Both are related to the identifiable essence of Jesus Christ.

1 Cor. 15:49 Just as we have borne the **image** of the man of dust, we shall also bear the **image** of the man of heaven.

The "image" of this identifiable body is no longer indistinguishable among the crowd but lives above us, in heaven. His resurrected body becomes the mark of a new spiritual identity. And through his Ascension Jesus Christ, in his **heavenly body,** rises to the full view of all. It becomes the ultimate miracle, the greatest of all visible **signs.**

That he has "risen from the dead" is a victory over the state of remaining in the **shadow** of nothingness. Therefore, the former condition of the **dead,** described as the meaningless state of the shadows of the powerless, is transcended with the resurrection.

The presence of the angel standing outside the tomb is further evidence of the good news about Christ's heavenly condition. The angels, from the Hebrew *mal'akh* which means **messenger,** are an additional link to the Old Testament. The angels were messengers of the LORD to Abraham, Isaac, Jacob, and Moses.[32] Similarly, the angel becomes the **medium** of Christ the LORD to his followers.

•

Like Job he was abandoned by all, even God. Defender of the outcasts, he dies like one himself. Both typify the innocent servant who suffers for the sake of truth. Job's suffering enables him to see God, while Jesus dies to be God.

Jesus Christ is the **prototype** of a new humanity.

Like Job, he is a scapegoat singled out by society. This isolation enables Job to have a vision of God he could not conceive before. On the other hand, Jesus is God because he gave his life for that truth. Love and knowledge about God is now accessible through him. His resurrected body is a visible sign, the **door** to his realm. It enables the **powerless** to have access to the power of God despite the entrenched powers of the world.

Although Jesus is loved by many, his adversaries are plenty. At the end, they overcome him. Even though he chastised the hypocrisy of the Pharisees, he did not condemn their religion. As much as he opposed the merchants in the temple, he did not oppose commerce. He complained about the unfaithfulness of the cities, but he did not repudiate social order. He simply proclaimed that the powers of this world have no jurisdiction over his realm. His people obey a different set of laws and are governed by the power of love.

Jn. 13:13 You call me Teacher and Lord; and you are right, for so I am. If I then, your Lord and Teacher, have washed your feet, you also ought to wash one another's feet. For I have given you an example, that you also should do as I have done to you. Truly, truly, I say to you, a servant is not greater than his master; nor is he who is sent greater than he who sent him.

The real purpose of the miracle of the resurrection lies on the

---

[32] Gen. 18:1; 24:7; 31:11; Ex. 3:2.

responsibility that Christ gave to his followers. Herein lies the cost of discipleship.[33]

> Mt. 28:18 And Jesus came and said to them, ''All authority in heaven and on earth has been given to me. Go therefore and make disciples of **all nations,** baptizing them in the **name** of the **Father** and of the **Son** and of the **Holy Spirit,** teaching them to observe all that I have commanded you; and lo, I am with you always, to the close of the age.''

---

[33] Dietrich Bonhoeffer, The Cost of Discipleship, London, SCM Press Ltd, 1971.

THE HOLY SPIRIT: The Profane Vitality of the Trinity

W e have dealt with two of the persons of the Trinity in the former chapters. In order to complete the triune essence of God, we will now focus our attention on the Holy Spirit. Among the three, its identity is the most evanescent.

•

The Spirit is the most enduring epithet of God. We can find it from the first verses of Genesis to the last pages of the Book of revelation.

In the Old Testament, the Spirit is portrayed as the vitalizing force behind God's activity. The word *rûah*—spirit—in Hebrew, means "wind".[1]

The words spirit and breath are also linked in a special fashion to the creation of the world. As related in Genesis, God "breathes" his Spirit into "man" and **gives him life.**[2] Breathing suggests the physical act of inhaling and exhaling the wind. It also depicts the inner and outer omnipresent reality of the "Spirit of God" in nature. As such, the life giving Spirit alludes to the unfathomable mystery of the origin of life.

---

[1] In ancient Near East, the wind was regarded as the mysterious force associated with fertility, and the bringer of life. See Walter Eichrodt, Theology of the Old Testament, vol. 1, London, SCM Press, 1967, 46.

[2] See Gen. 1:2; 2:7; 6:3; Ps. 33:6; 104:99f; 146:4; Job 12:10; 27:3; 34:14f; Ezek. 37:7-10.

The concept of a deity breathing life into "man" is not exclusive to Judaism and was prevalent in the ancient Near East. Similar Babylonian and Egyptian mythologies associate the "breathing" activity with the origin and animation of all life.

Although the Old Testament uses the epithet "Spirit of God", it does not speak of the Holy Spirit *per se*. The appellative Spirit of God became popular in late Old Testament narratives to replace the name of God by its attributes. The epithet did not infer the idea that the Spirit was a "person" either. Nevertheless, the meaning of Spirit of God and Holy Spirit are synonymous, since one meaning of the word "holy" is "of God". Only in the New Testament narratives did the Holy Spirit take an identity of its own.[3]

In the Scriptures, the Spirit of God became the **inspiration** given to prophets **called** to speak the word of God.[4] In this sense, the presence of the Spirit is akin to the unfathomable ways in which the wind, of which the prophet is filled, blows in the desert. Similarly, speaking gives the unvocalized Hebrew alphabet meaning and sense.

> Ezek. 1:28 Such was the appearance of the likeness of the glory of the LORD. And when I saw it, I fell upon my face, and I heard the voice of one speaking. And he said to me "Son of man, stand upon your feet, and I will **speak** with you." And when he spoke to me, the **Spirit** entered into me and set me upon my feet; and I **heard** him speaking to me.

The Spirit infuses the gift of understanding and communication. Without this gift, the prophet would not be able to understand the word or message of God: in the Spirit of the Word lies the essence of all meaning.

Similarly, Mary is filled with the presence of the Spirit and understands the full extent of the message of God in regards to the virginal conception of her son Jesus Christ.

In Isaiah, the Spirit of God is linked in a special way with the covenant.[5] The original expectations of the Spirit of God were mainly centered on the physical strength and power of Israel, espe-

---

[3] See Yves M.J. Congar, The Word and the Spirit, San Francisco, Harper & Row Publishers, 1986; also, I Believe in the Holy Spirit, vol. 1 to 3, New York, The Seabury Press, 1983; and, Esprit de l'Homme, Esprit de Dieu, Paris, Les Editions du Cerf, 1983.

[4] The Hebrew word for prophet is *nabi'* which is translated into "called". 1 Sam. 10:6; 16:14; Hos. 9:7; Ezek. 2:2; 3:12f.

[5] Is. 59:21.

cially in the heroic exploits of war. These hopes were successively transformed into a more messianic message of salvation.

•

John the Baptist, in the Gospels, is paralleled to the prophets of the Old Testament when he acknowledges the presence of the Holy Spirit descending as a dove on Jesus at his baptism, John understands the presence of the Spirit of God in Jesus.

Jesus' birth, baptism, and resurrection all share the presence of the Holy Spirit. All three are symbols of **conception** and **rebirth.** At the baptism, the Father and the Holy Spirit are present revealing the Trinity at work. They all bear witness to the power of God's self **communication** as the **Word** becomes **flesh** in Jesus Christ. The Incarnation is the proof of the ongoing relationship between the Father, the Son, and the Holy Spirit.

At the baptism, the Holy Spirit is described in all four Gospels as a **dove** descending from heaven.[6] The symbol of the dove is a privileged metaphor that describes the essence and identity of the Holy Spirit. It is a symbol rich in significance even in the Old Testament.

The doves referred to in the Scriptures are of two species: the turtledove and the young pigeon. The Hebrew word *yona* is a general designation for various species of doves that lived in the Middle-East.

In the Old Testament, the dove is mentioned in the flood as bringing back a "freshly plucked olive leaf" to confirm that the land is now safe and **fertile** again.[7]

A popular character of the Old Testament also bears the name *Yona;* ie, Jonas. The word literally means, moaner. This is the same Jonas who was swallowed up by the whale and spit out three days later: an allegory that parallels the inside of the whale to the **womb** in which the hero undergoes the mythical journey of death and rebirth.

The dove is also paralleled to the sacrificial offerings. In Leviticus, the law prescribes the offering of two turtledoves or two young pigeons for a woman's purification after **childbirth.**[8] One bird is set aside as a burnt offering and the other for sin offering. These doves are prescribed as substitutes when the woman "cannot afford" the sacrifice of the more expensive lamb, further correlating the dove with the poor.

---

[6] Mt. 3:16; Mk. 1:10; Lk. 3:22; Jn. 1:32.

[7] Gen. 8:11.

[8] See also, Lk. 2:24; Lev. 1:14; 12:1-8.

Isa. 38:14 Like a swallow or a crane I clamour,
I moan like a dove.
My eyes are weary with looking upward.
O Lord, I am oppressed; be thou my security![9]

•

In the symbolic representations of Old Europe, the dove was associated with the Goddess.[10] In ancient Near East, the bird was usually identified with the chief female goddess of fertility. In the temple of Ishtar, the dove was connected to the goddess, and the prostitutes who participated in the cults were called the "doves of the temple". The dove was also known to represent the goddess Aphrodite.[11] We know from the writings of Homer that Athena and Hera also assumed the guise of the dove.

Because of the widespread influence of Hellenism in Palestine in Jesus' times, the four Evangelists must have been aware that the dove was the symbol of the goddess Aphrodite. The New Testament was written in *koine,* a Greek language. It was commonly spoken throughout Palestine during the time the Evangelists wrote the Gospels. In light of this, might it be possible that their representation of the dove as a metaphor for the Holy Spirit was meant to suggest a connection to the Goddess principle?

Mt. 10:16 . . . so be wise as **serpents** and innocent as **doves.**[12]

•

The Holy Spirit's presence at Mary's conception of Christ inaugurates his own sacred identity.

Later, Jesus is depicted as being "full of the Holy Spirit". He is led by the Spirit to the desert to fast for forty days, at the end of which period he is tempted by the devil. A parallel is made to the people of Israel's own journey in the wilderness. When he returns to Galilee, he comes back with the "**power** of the Spirit".

At the end of his public life, Christ tells his disciples that he will send another "Counselor" as soon as he leaves this world. The narratives use the word "paraclete" which is taken from the Greek

---

[9] The Old Testament links the symbol of the dove to the poor and the oppressed.

[10] See, Marija Gimbutas, The Language of the Goddess, San Francisco, Harper & Row, 1989, 318-319.

[11] Erwin R. Goodenough, Jewish Symbols in the Greco-Roman Period, vol. 8; Pagan Symbolism in Judaism, New York, Pantheon Books, 1958, 27-46.

[12] Although the quote which is attributed to Jesus may appear at first hand innocuous, it is in fact an older Syrian aphorism which invokes the attributes of the God and the Goddess. See Barbara G. Walker, The Woman's Encyclopedia of Myths and Secrets, San Francisco, Harper & Row, 1983, 252-254.

parakletos meaning helper, intercessor, and advocate. This Counselor is present at all times, ready to teach and guide "into all truth". He is described as another entity with a "mode of being" all of his own, distinct from the Father's and the Son's. And although he has a life of his own, he shares the same divine substance as God.

> Mt. 28:19 Go therefore make disciples of all nations, baptizing them in the name of the Father and of the Son and the Holy Spirit.

Baptism is the most celebrated symbol of spiritual rebirth. In the quote above, Jesus' last words give his apostles the authority to baptize in the name of the three persons of the Trinity. He also **breaths** on them the Holy Spirit. The same gift of life given to Adam by God at the beginning.

•

The synoptic accounts end with Jesus' crucifixion and resurrection. More evidence of the life of the Spirit is found in the Acts of the Apostles to fulfill the promise Jesus had made to his followers.

At the Pentacost, the additional **sign** of the presence and identity of the Holy Spirit manifests itself as all the disciples are gathered in an upper room where **Mary** the mother of Jesus is also present. Luke takes special care to mention that a group of **women** who followed Jesus throughout his public life, and who remained in the **shadow** of the male disciples, are there as well. Suddenly, a "mighty wind" fills the room and "tongues of fire" appear on every single one of them. Everybody is swiftly filled by the power of the Holy Spirit. They soon realize that they can speak in "other tongues". The Paraclete vented to them the gift of **communication.** but most important of all, the Holy Spirit provided them with the power of Christ's authority.

> Acts 4:13 Now when they saw the **boldness** of Peter and John, and perceived that they were **uneducated, common men,** they wondered; and they recognized that they had been with Jesus.

•

It is through the Holy Spirit that the disciples spread the Word to small groups of *ecclesiae* who began to diffuse throughout Palestine and Rome.[13] These early Christians, who were for the most

---

[13] Which translated into assemblies or the more common churches and the Church.

part Jews, believed in the impending return of Christ and the imminent fall of the empire. Neither materialized.

Their faith remained steadfast despite the Roman persecution. They were unaware that unforseeable events would soon favor their faith to expand throughout the Roman empire.

One of these events was the sudden conversion of Constantine, in 312 AD. Constantine apparently witnessed the sight of a luminous cross in the sky. The vision had a message attached to it which read: *In hoc signo vinces;* eg, "With this sign you will win". He ordered that the symbol of the cross be put on all of his soldiers' shields. The battles he fought and won afterwards strengthened his belief on the benefit of this emblem symbolizing the new faith. As soon as he became Emperor, he made Christianity the official religion of Rome.

As the Church flourished, it spread to the limits of the Roman empire and beyond. Church officials soon gathered in councils to resolve matters of faith and doctrine in order to dispel a number of heresies that were emerging among the believers. During the councils of Nicaea (AD 325) and Constantinople (AD 382), the creed of the Holy Spirit was promulgated. At these councils, the Holy Spirit was defined as "the LORD, the **giver of life**".[14]

---

[14] This creed also states that the Holy Spirit spoke through the Prophets.

THE MOTHER OF GOD: The Overshadowed Reality of the Goddess

Archaeological findings show that the earliest and most prevalent type of artifacts discovered in Old Europe show an overwhelming concern with female symbolism. They were, in all probability, connected to some form of cultic origin or purpose.[1] The discovery of sculptured images and cave paintings of female figures from numerous sites, some dating as far back as twenty five thousand years, reveals a pervasive interest in female artistic representation that suggests some form of **Goddess** worship. One typical example of the earliest expressions of these figurines was found in the region of Dordogne, France, it depicts a **pregnant woman.** These little statues, also called **Venuses**—named after the Roman goddess of love—outnumber their male counterparts ten to one.

These discoveries have a tremendous implication on the theories of the origin and development of the earliest forms of religious beliefs and mythological expressions. According to the archaeological data, these female cultic representations appear to have been pervasive during most of the prehistory of Old Europe. Although archaeologists and anthropologists do not agree on a single theory to explain these discoveries, they nevertheless recognize that they reveal the basis of an elaborate system of cultic life in connection with attributes associated with the Goddess.

---

[1] See Marija Gimbutas, The Language of the Goddess, San Francisco, Harper and Row, 1989.

A great number of the figurines, though not all, are early evidence of fertility cults linked to the emergence of agriculture. The sheer abundance of these Venuses confirms nevertheless, an overwhelming feminine presence in the cultural and religious life of prehistoric cultures.

These artifacts represent a wide variety of female functions such as, maturation, menstruation, copulation, pregnancy, birth, and lactation. These goddesses came in different shapes and forms. In some instances, they are represented by animal forms like a **snake** or a **bird.** Among the air and water deities some are believed to be cosmic symbols of regeneration and life. Other cases show the figurines as faceless, nude, and corpulent. Others represent women with enormous breasts, buttocks, and protruding abdomens. While the more common ones show women in an advanced stage of pregnancy.

What is most interesting about these discoveries is the consistency and continuity with which these cults evolved from the early stages of history. Gradually, the Goddess' symbolism developed into a complex symbolism of human needs. They presumably arose with the development of agriculture and domestication, and are believed to be responsible for the development of a more complex form of social organization.

It is during the "Neolithic Revolution" that we begin to see signs of humans mastering their natural environment. Slowly, the main forms of subsistence evolved from hunting and food gathering, to agriculture and the domestication of herd animals.[2]

Foremost, the Goddess has been associated with the fertility cults. Although the survival of the species must have been a central concern of the fertility cults, these goddesses were also, in a broader sense, "life creators", a symbol of **renewal** and socio-cultural **regeneration.** It is probable that these symbols reflect an important stage in the evolution of symbolic representation of culture in general. As Marija Gimbutas points out, the **Great Goddess** is much more than a mere fertility goddess.[3] She played an essential part in the development of religious symbolism and culture.

The Goddess cannot be dispelled as only a stage in the evolutionary process, but must be recognized as a fundamental aspect of the primal representation of the human *psyche,* which Mircea Eliade calls **archetypes.**[4] These discoveries demand a closer scrutiny and a greater attention. They are an indispensable key to fully

---

[2] James Mellaart, Earliest Civilizations of the Near East, New York, McGraw-Hill, 1965.

[3] Marija Gimbutas, Ibid., 316-317.

[4] Mircea Eliade, Cosmos and History, New York, Harper Torchbooks, 1959.

understanding the past and present religious and mythological world we live in.

And as we have already outlined, the Goddess' profane reality has been deliberately overshadowed in the Bible. For this reason alone, the continuous study of the primal essence of her being is important. If one takes notice of the growing interest and the ever greater number of books on the subject, her obscurity may only be temporary. And if the momentum persists, we might find the key to unraveling the **whole** reality of human spirituality.

•

Between the fifth and fourth millennia BC, the peaceful, sedentary and agricultural societies of Old Europe, in which the Great Goddess, it is believed, played a major role, began to endure the invasion of nomadic patriarchal tribes. The warrior mentality of "the god(s)" worshippers began to challenge the Goddess' dominion and they began to impose their own cults.[5] One possible scenario is that, in time, none of the goddesses retained their supremacy; they were forced into subservience and cast into oblivion.

As centuries passed and as the major cultures of ancient Near East like Egypt and Sumer developed, the Goddess' worship retained some of its popularity as she shared equal devotion with her male counterparts. In the semi-nomadic tribes of Israel, however, the Goddess was undergoing a propaganda campaign to completely eradicate her reality from their cultic practices. Back then, women were literally and legally the **property** of men who submitted to the tribal rule of the God of the fathers. These laws and practices reflected the exclusion of the Goddess principle from the cultic life of Israel: the God of Israel was believed to be the only superior God, no other god could be worshiped except Him. In the process, "monotheism" thrived at the expense of other gods and goddesses.

We have seen in Genesis and all through the text of the Pentateuch how critical it became to control the progeny through the dominion of women's fertility. The female's sexuality had to be checked and maintained under male authority so to preserve the racial origin of the offspring. Women's behavior was closely regulated by the patriarchal laws, in stark contrast with more ancient matrilineal cultures where life in society was ruled by the legitimacy of the mother's offspring regardless of who the father was.

As the community life developed into more complex forms of social organization, the symbolic manifestations of the gods and

---

[5] The abundant discoveries of that period's arms may help corroborate and justify such a theory.

goddesses evolved as well. Cosmologies became more elaborate as they reflected a more complex form of the socio-cultural life they depicted.

From the early stages of prehistory to the emergence of more developed cultures, worship of the Goddess remained more or less pervasive. Although she may have assumed different identities, her essence remained basically the same. Many such goddesses in the ancient Near East were extremely popular and could be found in the most important cultures at the dawn of history.

Among them is Asherah, a Canaanite goddess, the tree symbol in Genesis.

The 1929 discovery of the Ugarit tablets in Ras Shamra, Syria, enabled scholars to decipher that Athirat, of which Asherah is a dialectical variant, is described as the wife of El, the chief god of the Ugaritic pantheon. While El is described as the "God", the "strong, powerful one", the "father", and the "creator of creatures", Athirat is portrayed as the "creatress of the gods".[6] As we have mentioned, El is one of the most ancient references to the semitic God.

The presence of Asherah in the Bible has provoked considerable scholarly debate. This goddess was worshipped by the Canaanites, a people who spoke a Semitic language in the area that is commonly known today as Palestine and Israel. At different periods of Israel's history, the Goddess was also revered by the Hebrews to the great consternation of the prophets. Ample evidence of her influence is related in the Bible.

One particular episode of Israel's history is revealing. Following the secession of the northern kingdom of Israel from the southern kingdom of Judah, during Jeroboam's reign, Asherah was worshipped in the temple of Jerusalem as late as 586 BC. Even Solomon, who built the temple, worshipped Asherah.[7]

The Goddess is a blend of several Near Eastern goddesses: among them, the Canaanites Athirat and Astarte, the Egyptians Qudshu and Anat, as well as the Mesopotamian goddesses Inanna and Ishtar. Asherah was a giver of life and a symbol of fertility, and her cult involved some form of temple prostitution.

The extent to which this particular form of worship had influ-

---

[6] A common trait of the divinities of the time is that the male gods tended to represent a reality statically, whereas their female consorts were thought of as bringing that reality into action. See William J. Fulco, SJ., The Canaanite God Resep, New Haven, American Oriental Society, 1976.

[7] 1 Kings 11:5; 15:13; 2 Kings 17:16f.

enced and penetrated Judaism can be seen in details in Biblical texts themselves.[8]

2 Kings 17:16 And they forsook all the commandments of the LORD their God, and made for themselves molten images of two calves; and they made an Ashe'rah, and worshipped all the hosts of heaven, and served Ba'al.

•

Asherah, in the Old Testament, mostly refers to a cultic place or to objects in the form of a wooden stela representing a tree. The tree, as we have outlined, is a predominant symbol of the creation myth of Genesis. These upright pillars, usually carved with inscriptions, were for the most part symbols of human and agricultural fertility. These sculptured wooden images set in the ground next to the god Baal were located on hilltops.[9]

The Asherah was an important household cult. Numerous small clay figurines of nude women were found all over Palestine. They can be dated from all ages of the Israelite period. These nude clay figurines were kept for private use by the worshippers. Several of these are typical representations of Asherah shown as a woman with protruding breasts. According to this evidence, the worship of the goddess must have been popular among all segments of Hebrew society. The cult, it seems, did not meet serious opposition until the end of the Israelite monarchy.

Asherah was known to the Hebrews since the first settlement in Canaan, after the exodus. Having to depend on agriculture as a means of survival, they probably also turned to the local customs related to the fertility cults, of which Asherah was a predominant goddess.

There is no such thing as a Hebrew goddess in the Bible. There is, however, ample evidence of a strong **opposition** to her cult. There are numerous passages attesting to the **threat** that the Goddess posed to Yahweh.

Among the many interesting accounts that reveal the presence of Asherah, is the episode in the royal court of Israel during the reign of King Ahab (873-852 BC). He had married Jezebel, the daughter of the king of Sidon, in order to cement an alliance with her father.

---

[8] The name Asherah with the more commonly masculine plural Asherim was used in the Bible. See also Kings 18:17-19; 1 Kings 14:23; 2 Kings 13:6; 21:7, 23:6f; Jeremiah 7:17-18; 44:17-25, etc.

[9] See Raphael Patai's chapter on Asherah in, The Hebrew Goddess, New York, Avon Books, 1978.

Acting under her influence, King Ahab built an altar to Baal in Samaria and "made" an Asherah.[10] In Sidon, Asherah had been worshipped for at least five centuries prior to that. Evidence of her popularity is reflected by the number of guests that are said to have been invited at a feast. On that occasion, the king's court was filled with 450 prophets of Baal, and 400 prophets of Asherah. The intrusion of these aliens infuriated the prophet Elijah who challenged the Baal prophets to a rain-making contest. The Canaanite god was defeated in a violent uproar led by Elijah and his people. Yahweh was vindicated. Although the account mentions the slaughter of all of Baal's prophets, there is no word of the outcome of Asherah's prophets. Why were they spared Yahweh's wrath? One explanation could be that she was a popular deity among the people. Perhaps, as David Noel Freedman suggests, Yahweh defeated Baal to take Asherah as his own consort.[11]

2 Kings 13:6 . . . the Ashe'rah also remained in Samar'ia.

Although Asherah was a predominant figure, other goddesses were also popular; among them, Astarte, also called Anat, the daughter of Asherah and El. Although Astarte is mentioned 9 times in the Bible compared to 40 times for her mother, she nevertheless surpassed her mother in popularity during certain periods of history. The name Astarte means literally the **womb,** and she was often called "she of the womb". The name is in itself revealing. She, like her mother, was a goddess of fertility, and her brother and consort, was the symbol of male fertility. They were known as the divine couple, and as the **begetters.**

There are abundant archaeological discoveries that link Egyptian and Canaanite divinities. The discovery at the malachite mines of Serabit el Khadim, on the Sinai Peninsula in Egypt, reveals a similarity between the Goddess' cults in Canaan and Egypt. Numerous small relief plaques have been found in these areas on which the image of the goddess Astarte bears a very close resemblance to the Egyptian images of Isis and Hathor. The latter was also called "the Lady of the Sycamore", a common representation that links the symbol of the tree to Asherah. These plaques, for the most part, were found marked with the inscription *quadosh*—holy. Albright

---

[10] 1 Kings 16:32-33; 18:19-40.

[11] See David Noel Freedman's, Yahweh of Samaria and His Asherah, in, *Biblical Archeologist,* December 1987, 249. In another event, the narrative describes how Asherah also escaped the Baalist massacre and the destruction of Baal's temple in Samaria during yet another Yahwist uprising.

observed that the Canaanite divinities might be more primitive than other forms of worship. He also noted that these Canaanite gods and goddesses have a "fluidity" of personality and function. In other words, these divinities can change physical shape and form, alter their relationships and identity with other divinities at will, and adopt names of other goddesses with incredible ease.[12]

As we explained, Yahweh emerged from a revelation in the desert. The exodus was the return to a semi-nomadic way of life similar to the herdsmanship of the Patriarchs before their move to Egypt. Furthermore, the journey toward the promised land was favorable neither for agriculture nor for the cults related to fertility, as evidenced by the manna, the food God sent from the sky. Yahweh thrived in the desert where the **isolation** helped to develop the fundamental precept of the **opposition** to **other** gods and Asherah.

Judg. 2:13 They forsook the LORD, and served the Ba'als and the Ash'taroth.[13]

The worship of the goddess Asherah was reported in the scriptures as continually **antagonizing** Yahweh.[14] The texts often refer to Astarte as *Ashtoreth,* a derogative name that implied shame.

1 Sam. 7:3 Then Samuel said to all the house of Israel, "If you are returning to the LORD with all your heart, then put away the foreign gods and the Ash'taroth from among you, and direct your heart to the LORD, and serve him only, and he will deliver you out of the hand of the Philistines." So Israel put away the Ba'als and the Ash'taroth, and they served the LORD only.

The commandment is very explicit. It does not allow the worship of any molten image or any goddess. Although the prohibition to worship any other gods does not exclusively refer to Asherah, the goddess of fertility is, without a doubt, a primal target. Was the first commandment specifically directed toward the popular goddess Asherah? One thing is certain, the goddess' worship was a threat to Yahweh's patriarchal precepts.

---

[12] William Foxwell Albright, Archeology and the Religion of Israel, Baltimore, The Johns Hopkins Press, 1968, 71 ff.

[13] Also: Judg. 10:6; 1 Sam. 7:3-4; 31:10.

[14] Judg. 2:13, 3:7; 1 Sam. 7:3-4.

What is remarkable about Exodus is that it remains, for the people of Israel, the most sacred event and the most sacred narrative. Everything in Judaism is centered around the text: Yahweh, Moses, the alliance, the commandments, the law, the ark, and the promised land. Most of the original religious experience stems from the revelation of Yahweh as a jealous God opposed to any other god.

Yet Judaism is not devoid of the feminine aspect of the divinity. The shekhinah is often used by the Talmudic tradition to describe a mystical presence of God. The concept eventually developed into a spiritual entity that personified a compassionate figure, mostly with feminine attributes, that sometimes argued with God in defense of the humans. The shekhinah was a mediating agent between the divine and the human. The Hebrew word *shekhinah* means "dwelling" or "resting place", but it is more commonly used in the sense of "presence". The word first appeared in early rabbinical literature as it referred to the divine presence in the tabernacle. It eventually came to signify God's presence among the people of Israel.

The rabbis believe that the shekhinah had a close and privileged relationship with Moses. According to the Talmudic tradition, the feminine companion was present from his childhood through his adult life, continually communicating with him. Moses even left his wife to be closer to his shekhinah.[15]

The Mother of God

The Gospels herald a new era. A transition from the Old tradition to the New. The Bible's emphasis on God of the Fathers is shifted to God the Son. The imageless features of the Father become visible in the Incarnation of the Word. The promised land of old is replaced by the quest for the kingdom of Heaven. The two kingdoms are visionary anticipations of an-**other** world created by the "Word".

The new Christian era also inaugurates new relationships: between the divine Father and his Son, but also between the Mother of God and her child Jesus.

The Incarnation brings forth the question of the birth of Jesus. Although John the Evangelist identifies the origin of Jesus with the **Word** in Genesis, Matthew and Luke relate the birth of Christ to his virgin Mother. Mary's motherhood is, henceforth, put in the foreground. In Genesis, "man's" inception is shaped by divine hands,

---

[15] The Talmud also associates the divine essence with the Spirit of God. Both expressions relate to God's presence and closeness with his people.

with the dust from the ground, then God **breathes** life into it, while the woman is an afterthought, ironically born of man's own flesh. In Matthew and Luke, however, Mary is the **matrix** of the Messiah's birth. Perhaps unconspicuously, the narratives open the door to Mary as the Mother of God, a symbolic link toward the primordial "Great Mother".

Except for the birth narratives, her image is **overshadowed** by her son's mission. Yet while Jesus speaks constantly of his absent Father, it is his mother who is present at the most crucial moments of his life. She conceives Jesus Christ with the spiritual intervention of the Holy Spirit. Jesus is born human through her, and divine through the Spirit; hence, the **Incarnation.** At Cana, Mary asks Jesus to perform his first miracle, the first of his **signs,** which inaugurates his public life. At his crucifixion, the culmination of her son's mission, she witnesses her son's whole life cycle: his birth, his mission, and his death. Her presence symbolizes her son's sacrifice as well as hers.

It is another Mary, however, that is present at Jesus' resurrection. It is Mary Magdalene, Jesus' loved one, who first sees the resurrected body of Christ. Finally, at the Pentecost, both Marys and all of the other disciples are reunited and are filled with the Holy Spirit.

Mary is described, in the Gospels, as the "mother of Jesus". Only later, at the Council of Ephesus in 431 AD, would she gain the title of *theotokos;* ie, the "Mother of God".

Ephesus, by a freak historical coincidence, was also the site of the most famous temples of Artemis. In Greek mythology, she was the goddess of chastity and of the hunt, similar to her Roman counterpart Diana. Although she is known as *parthenos,* as both maiden and virgin, she was also the goddess of childbirth. In many ways, Artemis also typifies the prehistoric archetype of the goddess of fertility and regeneration popular in Old Europe.

At the outset, Artemis was the prototype of the Great Goddess. Later, her role in Greek mythology was transformed into that of a virgin. This image of the maiden or the virgin could be seen as further evidence of the patriarchal interference and manipulation of women's sexuality in mythology.[16]

The title of "God's bearer", given to Mary at Ephesus, does not confer upon her the divine attribute of Goddess, even though the sacred affiliation to her Son gives her somewhat of a divine right. Although Christianity has no Goddess per se, the **Mother of God**

---

[16] Carol P. Christ, Symbols of Goddess and God in Feminist Theology, in, The Book of Goddess Past and Present, ed. by Carl Olson, New York, Crossroad, 1983, 231-251.

shares many of her attributes and functions. And despite the fact that Mary does not play a prominent role in the New Testament, her image has developed into a cult of great following and devotion. Mary's worship, especially if seen by non-Catholics, is in many ways comparable to a Goddess'.

The birth narratives are the most eloquent about Mary's identity.[17] It is through these texts that she has been immortalized as the Mother of God. It is that image that is most present in our minds. Foremost, the virginal conception has been the center of important theological debates, especially with the proclamation of the "Immaculate Conception" defined by Pius IX in 1854.[18]

The virginal birth of Jesus is one among many examples of the role that virginity plays in the world of mythologies. There are other parallels to be found among founders of other religions who were also born of virgins: Buddha, Krishna, the son of Zoroaster, and, in some versions, Zoroaster himself. In Greek and Roman mythologies, heros born to virgins are typified by Dionysos, Romulus and Remus. The concept of virginal birth can also be found in most ancient cultures like Egypt, Greece, Persia, and India. The concept is also prominent in the native North American cultures like the Inuit, the Apache, and the Navajo.

Most of the examples point to the heros whose mothers were virgin as a "sign" of their greatness, but not necessarily to the virginity *per se*. In other words, the fact that these heros were portrayed as being born to a virgin is a sign of their supernatural origin. In the language of myth, the supernatural quality of the heros is attested through a virgin mother as a **sign** that separates them from ordinary people. In a sense, the cause of their greatness might be connected to the unique and exclusive relationship they had with their mother. The **virginity** may be tied to the unconditional nature of the relationship between the mother and the child. It also infers the woman's independence and self-sufficiency in her role of mother. It suggests that the fertility is rooted in herself and is self-contained.

In mythology, there seems to be no apparent contradiction in the belief that a mother can also be a virgin. In order to understand the virginal conception, one has to see it in the light of mythological significance. As a specific form of language, myth deals in a metaphysical and metaphorical dimension. The physical world is differ-

---

[17] The Koran also makes some eloquent and reverential references to Mary (Surahs 3 and 19).

[18] Pius IX, Immaculate Conception, *Ineffabilis Deus,* DS 2803, issued December 8, 1854, Boston, St. Paul Books and Media.

entiated from **meta**physical as it relates to two distinct semantic realities. Such is the distinction between spiritual conception and the physical—or sexual—conception of Christ. Moreover, the word conception is equivocal. Both the physical and metaphysical sense can be implied. It allows for two types of relationships; between man and woman in procreation, and between mother and child in gestation.

The virginal conception depicts the relationship between Mother and Son as one of devotion, a unique and special spiritual bond, so to speak. It implies a dynamic revelation of the Holy Spirit by Mary in her conception of Christ. Her virginity relates more to her spiritual relationship with her Son than to a biological state or her sexual behavior with a father who remains in the background.[19] In other words, between mother and child, we can speak of a pure, spiritual, and unconditional love.

mother > child > virginity   = spiritual conception

woman > man > sexual relation = physical conception

The word **conception** should be understood here in the context of its two meanings. First, in the spiritual sense, as the faculty of conceiving in the mind. Second, as procreation, the action of conceiving in the womb. On one hand, the Virgin Mary, through the spiritual revelation of the Holy Spirit, conceived of Christ according to tradition. In this sense, the Holy Spirit is not to be understood as the male element in the intervention, but as God's presence which Mary acknowledges.[20] On the other hand, the birth of Jesus the man is biological, historical. Here, the parthenogenesis of Jesus underlines the unique relationship between Mary and Jesus. Both conceptions make up the mystery in which the "Son of man" and the "Son of God" meet in the Incarnation of Jesus/Christ, the Son/God.

Holy Spirit   > Virgin Mary > Christ

                                Jesus Christ

Mary's revelation > Mary's body > Jesus

---

[19] The narratives describe man's participation, as portrayed by Joseph, as secondary. Mary is described as "betrothed" to Joseph, but he did not "know" her—a word used to imply sexual union. Nevertheless, Joseph, by recognizing Jesus as his child though he was not his own, became his legal father according to Jewish law.

[20] In Hebrew, the word for spirit has a rather feminine connotation which corroborates, in this instance, Mary's "spiritual" act of conceiving God.

Another important event in Mariology took place in 1950 when Pope Pius XII defined the dogma of the Assumption of Mary. This dogma confirms that Mary, the virgin mother of God, was taken into **heaven** in body and soul.

The likeness between God's Mother and her divine Son, in the way of the nobility and dignity of body and soul—a likeness that forbids us to think of the **heavenly Queen** as being separated from the heavenly King—makes it entirely imperative that Mary "should be only where Christ is".[21]

The epithet **Queen of Heaven** is a title also shared by Astarte and Asherah.[22] Even though theological doctrine forbids any connection between the Virgin Mary and the pagan goddesses, it remains interesting that a similar name came up to describe the Mother of God. It just shows that the archetype of the Goddess principle is always present deep in the human *psyche*. If we compare some other attributes and names associated with the goddess we come up with this:

MARY	ASHERA
heavenly Queen	Queen of heaven
Mother of God	Creator of gods
mother of Jesus	fertility goddess

MARY	ASTARTE
conceived in her womb	Astarte, the womb

We have seen how the Goddess principle has been tentatively eradicated from the Old Testament and **overshadowed** in the New, until only a glimpse of her image could be perceived in the background. Throughout history her epithets and names may have changed, yet her essence remained the same.

The Church, in its own spiritual way, acknowledged her being since the mid-nineteenth century. In 1858, Mary appeared in Lourdes, France, where her Spirit performed numerous miracles. She appeared again in Fatima, Portugal, in 1917. And lately, visions

---

[21] Pius XII, Assumption, *Munificentissimus Deus,* DS 3903, issued November 1, 1950, Boston, St. Paul Books & Media, 15.

[22] Merlin Stone, When God Was a Woman, San Diego, Harvest/HBJ Book, 1976, 163 ff.

of her being have been reported in Medugorje, Yugoslavia. Her apparitions are **expressions** of a deep longing for her spiritual being and are signs of spiritual as well as political change.[23]

---

[23] As Karl Rahner points out, visions and apparitions must be interpreted as spiritual expressions of deep mystical feelings rather than inexplicable physical marvels. When the Church investigates the validity of such visions, for instance, it does not examine the physical evidence of the apparition but the spiritual trustworthiness of the people who experience such happenings. See, Karl Rahner's, Vision and Prophecies, London, Burns and Oates, 1963.

THE HOLY TRINITY & THE SACRED TRIAD:
The Sacred, the Profane, & the Wholly Other

The Holy Trinity is the most fascinating but also the most misunderstood of all theological doctrines. It's an unfortunate situation, because the Trinity may hold the key to understanding an important facet of the dynamic division inherent in all religious experience.[1]

The first principle of the doctrine stipulates that the Trinity is an absolute mystery. Its revelation is only possible with the help of two spiritual activities: love and knowledge. With love, one is open to the fullest to life's mystery. Through love, we may live the Trinity, although we may not be able to express its mystery. With knowledge, life could be experienced with the greatest of insight. Yet words and symbols may be inadequate to describe the whole reality of the Trinity. Its mystery is only accessible through God's self-communication, which is a process of everlasting realization; herein lies the mystery.[2]

The Old Testament does not contain a doctrine of the Trinity *per se,* even though, in retrospect, it may appear to confirm it. For instance, the name Elohim implies a divine plurality. Furthermore,

---

[1] In that respect I share Raimundo Panikkar's view. See Raimundo Panikkar's, The Trinity and the Religious of Man, New York, Orbis Books, 1973, 42.

[2] Although I have studied Theology, I am not a theologian. I am not trying to develop a theory on the Trinity, I leave that to the theologians. I merely used the Trinity, which I believe to be the most important theological doctrine of Christianity, as an analogy to the sacred, the profane, and the wholly other.

the LORD appears to Abraham under the guise of "three men" who tell the skeptical patriarch that his wife Sarah will **bear** a son despite her advanced age.[3]

The Bible says that there is one God, yet God is not alone. He created man in his image in order to communicate his creation to him. In the same fashion, he created woman so that man would not be alone. Therefore, God needs an interlocutor with whom to talk. As the narratives show, God chose to speak to Moses and his prophets. Yahweh reveals himself to whomever he chooses in order to establish a relationship with his people throughout history.

With the Gospels, the Trinity is inaugurated. The narratives recount the story of Jesus who speaks of his Father, but also of the Holy Spirit. This development introduced a new dimension to the reality of God.

Throughout the centuries, the Church developed the doctrine apologetically. Most of it has been developed during the first fifteen centuries of the Church's history. It has remained basically the same for the last five hundred years.

Not until late in the fourth century did the Church's teaching begin to take shape.[4] The fundamental tenets developed by the magisterium define the Trinity as an absolute mystery and believe that one God exists in three persons: they are equal, coeternal and omnipotent.[5] God is one divine nature, one essence, and one substance. In the Trinity, the three persons are distinct from one another. The Father has no principle of origin. The Son is born from the substance of the Father. The Spirit is not begotten, but proceeds from the Father and the Son, from one principle, in one single spiration; eg, action of breathing.

As the definition above shows, the Trinity is a complex doctrine, rendered even more difficult by the elaborate lexicon developed by the magisterium over the ages. Yet, in order to understand any of its basic tenets, one must first comprehend a fundamental concept, that of "person".

In the Old Testament, the word "person" —*nepes* in Hebrew— has a broad range of meanings which includes: living being, soul,

---

[3] Gen. 18:2f.

[4] Doctrines on the Trinity have been developed during the Council of Nicaea (325 AD), the first Council of Constantinople (381 AD), the Eleventh Council of Toledo (675 AD), the Fourth Lateran Council (1215 AD), the Second Council of Lyons (1274 AD) and the Council of Florence (1439-45 AD). Other important documents that relate to the doctrine are the Apostles' Creed, Nicene Creed, Athanasian Creed, and Paul VI's Confession of Faith.

[5] The magisterium dictates that God exists in three persons, subsistences, hypostases. These terms were used to distinguish the dual nature of Christ as divine and human. Karl Rahner, SJ, Divine Trinity, in Sacramentum Mundi v. 6, Montreal, Palm Publishers, 1970, 295-303.

breath. In several instances, it is similar to "adam".[6] The New Testament uses the Greek translation of the word *anthropos* which has basically the same meaning. In the course of history, the Church developed the concept of "person" gradually to reflect the more complex definitions of the Incarnation and the Trinity.

Foremost, the word **person** is not used in the psychological sense of independent center of consciousness or personal center of action.[7] The persons of the Trinity, in these terms, would imply three states of consciousness with three free wills, which is not only misleading but incorrect. The persons of the Trinity are not three different centers of activity.

Person is not understood as a separate physical entity, but more as Karl Rahner describes it, as a "distinct manner of being". Therefore, each of the three persons is not separate, they are selfless and complementary, where God is **one** essence and **one** absolute self-presence. There are not three consciousness either, but rather **one** spiritual and absolute reality that subsists in a threefold manner of being.[8]

The concept of person, although somewhat confusing and vague, is nevertheless necessary. It is useful because it allows us to fathom the idea of relationship, from which **communication** stems. More precisely, God's dynamic **self-communication.** In this sense, the three persons are fully and totally open to each other as a unity, as One God.

If we replace the word "person" by "modes of being", as suggested by Karl Barth, or, "distinct manners of being", as proposed by Karl Rahner, we gain clarity in respect to the threeness of God, but lose in terms of the dynamic tri-unity inherent in one God. The image of person is retained because it is easier to envision God in

---

[6] Gen. 46:18f; Ex. 1:5 etc.

[7] In theological terms, person implies *individuum vagum* or vague being. Karl Rahner describes "person" as a "rational subsistent"; ie, a rational being existing substantially or really of or by itself. In trying to clarify the concept he alternatively uses "way of subsistence" or "distinct manner of subsisting". Equivalent expressions have been proposed by Karl Barth who has suggested the words "modes of being". They are mostly used to clarify the distinctness of each person while maintaining their unity in one God so to avoid the trap of tritheism. See Karl Rahner, SJ, The Trinity, New York, Herder & Herder, 1970, 111, and, Divine Trinity, in Sacramentum Mundi, Montreal, Palm Publishers, 1970, 295-308. Also, Karl Barth, Church Dogmatics vol. 1, The Doctrine of the Word of God, Part One, Edingburgh, T&T Clark, 1975, 348 f.

[8] A further analogy might be in order, although it might be viewed as too "modernistic". At the time when conception actually occurs, there are three distinct genetic entities that coexist: the egg from the mother, the spermatozoid from the father, and the embryo, which become the child's new genetic entity. We might say that the three genetic "persons" are distinct, yet they are one human being.

terms of a person rather than a "mode of being" or a "distinctive manner of being".[9]

Therefore, the person exists only in terms of relationships. Personality exists only as interpersonality. In the Old Testament, the person exists foremost in relations of the I-Thou-we kind.[10] The case in point is the relationship between God, Moses, and Israel as revealed in the Bible. However, the relationship expounded by Martin Buber is characteristic of the Old Testament's theological tradition of God's condescending majesty, emphasizing the otherness of God, whereas the concept of the Trinity, as expounded in the New Testament, is Christological. It presents the relation as of the me-you-we type. Jesus, as the God incarnate, reached out to the profane realm: the here and now. His relationship with the world is transformed into a more mundane kind. As a result, he breaks the master/servant relationship between God and his creation, between the land-LORD and his servant.[11]

●

Jn. 1:1 In the beginning was the **Word,**
and the Word was with **God,**
and the Word was God.
He was in the beginning with God;
all things were made through him,
and without him was not anything made that was
made.
In him was **life.**
and the life was the light of men.
The light shines in the darkness,
and the darkness has not overcome it.[12]

---

[9] The magisterium further states that there are three distinct relations and properties in God. There is also a distinction between the essence of God and the relations that constitute the persons. The "relative" persons in God are not really distinct from the essence of God and, therefore, do not form a quaternity. In God, all is one, except where an **opposition** of relationship exists. Each of the divine persons is fully in each other, and each of them is one true God. The divine persons cannot be divided from one another, in being or in operation. They form only a single principle of action. Their activity is one and the same even though only the Logos became "man".

[10] See, Martin Buber, I and Thou, New York, Scribners, 1970.

[11] In the English language the capital "I" implies a sense of majesty of the subject, characteristic of the Anglo-Saxon mentality, which is not present, say, in French or Italian.

[12] Taken from The Jerusalem Bible. The word "overcome" is better rendered into understand or grasp.

In the New Testament, communication of the **Word** is only possible through a medium of which Jesus is the prototype. The unfathomable presence of God's spoken Word in Genesis becomes incarnate in the Son through the life given by the Spirit in Mary.

God literally spoke the world into existence. Without the Word, God could not be heard or known. Man and woman are created in his "image" and bear witness to his Word and creation, emphasizing the possibility of a relationship between the Word and the **hearer.**[13]

Furthermore, God shares his knowledge and his love through the Word in a twofold manner. God reveals himself through the "economic" Trinity, which discloses itself in history, and through the "immanent" Trinity, which **inspires** the Spirit of the Word to the hearer.[14]

ONE GOD
The Trinity

economic	*immanent*
the Trinity as	the three persons
it reveals itself	in relation to
to the world and	each other
history	

---

[13] See Karl Rahner's, Hearer's of the Word, Montreal, Palm Publishers, 1969, and, Luis Alonso Schokel's, S.J., The Inspired Word, Montreal, Palm Publishers, 1965.

[14] Additional clarification about the meaning of "economy" may be necessary. Originally, the word meant the divine government of the world until Voltaire and his contemporaries began using the word with its modern sense. A devout anticleric, he, in all probability, used the word as an act of defiance toward the Catholic Church. Since we are on this subject, something else comes to my mind. I have noticed the frequent use of the word "theology" by the economist John Kenneth Galbraith. Although I fail to understand the exact meaning he confers to the word, he may also be inaugurating a new use for it.

In essence, the "economic" and "immanent" Trinity are one dynamic reality breathing life into each other. The "immanent" Trinity could not subsist without the "economic" Trinity, and vice versa. Similar in fashion to the Spirit, as the breath and the wind that is breathed in and out, reflecting the inner and outer mystery of God.

Mt. 28:19 "Go therefore and make disciples of **all nations, baptizing** them in the name of the **Father** and of the **Son** and of the **Holy Spirit** . . ."[15]

The sacred triad: the sacred

We have already outlined the three principles of the religious experience in terms of the sacred, the profane, and the wholly other. At this point, we will parallel their definitions in analogy to the Trinity.

It is practically impossible to talk about the sacred without referring to the profane, since the identity of the first depends on its opposition to the second.

sacred	vs	*profane*
God	vs	Satan
holy	vs	common
pure	vs	impure
clean	vs	unclean

This dynamic opposition is the realm of religion. At this point, we must clarify that the "experience" of the religious must be distinguished from the interpretation of the experience. While the experience of the sacred is unique, the expression of that experience belongs to the field of language. Language relates the experience with the use of words and symbols, either spoken or written.[16]

Individuals experience the sacred everyday in varied forms: through the ecstasy of love, a revelation, nirvana, or even a UFO sighting. Although we may not understand or agree with a person's interpretation of his or her sacred experience, we cannot deny that he or she lived an extraordinary happening. His or her personal

---

[15] The scriptures tell us that the Son is sent by the Father, and the Spirit is sent by the Father and the Son. *Ergo,* the Father is the sender, the Son is the mediator, and the Holy Spirit is the **receiver.** Jn. 3:17; 6:57.

[16] Of course the meaning of "language" encompasses much more. All forms of communication, linguistic or semiotic, could be categorized as such.

experience is unique, unfathomable, and even ineffable; ie, language may not be an adequate medium to communicate that experience.

An example may be helpful. Everybody has experienced a dream at one time or another in their sleep. And each person's dream is unique. When the dreamer relates his or her dream, he or she does so with the help of language. However, language cannot accurately translate the dream which involves the total visual and participative experience of the dreamer. Consequently, it would be better to say that a person lives a dream. In relating his or her dream, the dreamer makes a linguistic account which is different than the original experience itself. In linguistics, the language of the dream is the object-language, whereas the account is a metalanguage. If a psychoanalyst, for instance, becomes involved with the interpretation of the dream, he or she is left only with an account of the dream of which the dreamer is the mediator. As such, the interpretation rendered through language is an obstacle to the full experience and full content of the dream.

In the study of the sacred, we are faced with a similar problem. We can only interpret the expression of the sacred, never its unique experience since we deal only with words and symbols that relate to the sacred. Language only reveals one aspect of religious experience, albeit an important one. Nevertheless, by exploring the manifestations of the sacred, we gain insight into the fundamental composition of the religion phenomenon as it manifests itself in language.

•

The word **sacred** comes from the Latin *sacer.* The Romans used the word to describe what was under their gods' jurisdiction. When they referred to the *sacrum,* it implied the location where a ritual was performed; namely, the temple. The sacred place was also intrinsically tied to the cult. Both, place and cult, were closely circumscribed and distinct from the outside space called the *profanum.* The **profane** literally means the space outside the temple. Hence, *profanare* meant to bring the object of **sacrifice** "out" of the temple, transgressing the boundary between the sacred and the profane.

The Bible uses mostly the word **holy**—in Hebrew *qadosh*—instead of sacred which has a similar meaning.[17] The temple, but especially the Holy of Holies, is separate from the common space. Similarly, the ritual performed in the temple distinguishes the

---

[17] Assuming that the root *qd* means "to set apart". There is also the possibility that the root *qdsh,* related to the Akkadian *qadashu,* means "to become pure", and in that sense it has more of a ritualistic connotation. From the same root as the Hebrew word for holy—*qdsh*—the word qedesha is used to describe the prostitute consecrated to Astarte.

sacred from the profane activity.

Priests are especially privileged persons who can be designated as sacred. Jerusalem, but more specifically, the temple of Jerusalem, was the sacred place *par excellence* and the center of the world, as the Holy of Holies was at the center of the temple and the ark was at the center of the Holy of Holies.[18]

•

Ex. 3:1 Now Moses was keeping the flock of his father-in-law, Jethro, the priest of Mid'ian; and he led his flock to the west side of the wilderness, and came to Horeb, **the mountain of God.** And the angel of the LORD appeared to him in a flame of fire out of the midst of a bush; and he looked, and lo, the bush was burning, yet it was not consumed. And Moses said, "I will turn aside and see this great sight, why the bush is not burnt." When the LORD saw that he turned aside to see, God **called** to him out of the bush, "Moses, Moses!" And he said, "Here am I." Then he said, **"Do not come near;** put off your shoes from your feet, for the **place** on which you are standing is **holy** ground." And he said, "I am the God of your father, the God of Abraham, the God of Isaac, and the God of Jacob." And Moses hid his face, for he was **afraid** to look at God.

The passage above reveals a central aspect of the sacred. The place where the hierophany occurs is described as the "mountain of God". As we have outlined, the mountain is a privileged place where the sacred appears. It is a universal symbol found in the most important mythologies of the world.

The "appearance" of the angel of the LORD announces the coming of a hierophany. Moses' sighting confirms a mysterious event, although it is yet without meaning. God's words finally reveal the purpose of the apparition. At the outset, God sets the boundaries between the holy and the common ground. The holy imposes a distance that separates the divine from the human, the extra-ordinary from the ordinary, the sacred from the profane.

the holy	vs	the common
Israel	vs	outsiders[19]
priests	vs	ordinary men

---

[18] The Sabbath also typifies the special time consecrated to Yahweh. Objects like the ark, the priests' adornments, and certain animals, especially the sacrificial ones, are also prescribed as sacred.

[19] Ex. 30:32,33.

138

The power of the holy, which is Yahweh's exclusivity, is bestowed upon Moses, his spokesman. Moses is the only one to whom Yahweh reveals his name. Yet, by the same token, the people of Israel are also consecrated by Yahweh as a "holy people", a "holy nation", a "holy race".[20] Yahweh's identity and the identity of his people are consecrated and set apart from other gods and other people.

Lev. 20:26 You shall be **holy** to me; for I the LORD am **holy,** and have **separated** you from the peoples, that you should be mine.

The origin of the sacred is described in the text as stemming from the center flowing toward its periphery.[21] The whole process emanates around the holy at the center of which Yahweh's words are the source of everything. In order of importance, Yahweh is the **holy one,** followed by Moses as the prophet, then the priests, and finally the people, all into one single entity: Israel. The "holy people" becomes a social and religious entity which is set apart by Yahweh. He is holy, and so is Israel. God is **separated** from other gods and Israel is set **apart** from other people to become the matrix of their religious identity.

Hence, only Yahweh's words enable him to reveal the holy. Without his words, his will could not be known. It goes without saying that the spoken word cannot be separated from the written word, since the Bible is a literary work. Without the **written word,** the experience of the holy would not have been preserved. The Bible is the **medium** that is used to propagate the story of Israel. Without the priests and scribes that have written and preserved the sacred heritage, it would have been lost forever.

•

Mt. 17:1 And after six days Jesus took with him Peter and James and John his brother, and led them up a high mountain **apart.** And he was **transfigured** before them, and his face shone like the **sun,** and his garments became white as **light.** And behold, there appeared to them **Moses** and **Eli'jah,** talking with him. And Peter said to Jesus, "Lord, it is well that we are here; if you wish, I will make three booths here, one for you and one for Moses and one for Eli'jah". He was still speaking, when lo, a bright cloud **overshadowed** them, and a **voice** from the cloud said, "This is my beloved **Son,** with whom

---

[20] Ex. 19:6; Isa. 62:12; Ezra 9:2.

[21] Edward Shils, Center and Periphery, Chicago, University of Chicago Press, 1975, 17f.

I am well pleased; listen to him." When the disciples heard this, they fell on their faces, and were filled with **awe.** But Jesus came and touched them saying, "Rise, and have no **fear.**" And when they lifted up their eyes, they saw no one but Jesus only.

In Matthew, Mark, and Luke the account of the transfiguration is almost identical.[22] The parallels with the text in Exodus are striking. The similarities are abundant: the mountain as a sacred place, the holy ground that sets boundaries "apart", Jesus' face that shines like the sun, the voice of God which is heard from nowhere, the awe, and the fear. Similar also is God's manifestations of power displayed in the thundering, the lightning, and the fire shared with the hierophanies on Mount Sinai and on Mount Carmel.[23]

Furthermore, Jesus is seen talking with Moses and Elijah. His association with the two biblical heros is presumably meant to associate and connect Jesus with two of the most powerful and charismatic personalities of the Old Testament.

As we go further, the similarities begin to fade. The most notable difference being the appellation of Jesus as the Son of God. This affiliation shatters and redefines the biblical concept of the holy.

Except where Moses is Yahweh's mouth, none of the Patriarchs are identified with the Word of God. They are significantly **his** prophets, **his** people, in other words, they are God's instruments. None of them were called his sons. And although the idea of affiliation is prominent in the Old Testament, as typified by the title "God of your fathers", the relation is meant to confer the idea of the sovereignty and authority of the patriarchal lineage rather than that of sonship. Furthermore, the Gospels inaugurate the sonship of Jesus Christ as the holy.

Ex. 3:14: (Yahweh) I AM WHO I AM

Jn. 8:58: (Jesus) Before Abraham was, I AM[24]

Therefore, Jesus shares the exclusivity of God's sacred identity. As a human being he becomes a visible and identifiable image of God. As such, he transcends the first and second commandments given by Yahweh. And, by performing miracles on the Sabbath, he

---

[22] Mk. 9:2-8; Lk. 9:28-36.

[23] Ex. 20:18; 1 Kings 18.

[24] Jn. 8:24; 13:19.

transgresses yet another commandment. As a result, Jesus becomes a law onto himself. He breaks the boundaries of the sacred's exclusivity.[25]

Jn. 17:19 And for their sake I **consecrate** myself, that they also may be consecrated in **truth.**

The profane

As we have mentioned earlier, the profane is closely related to the sacred. The very existence of the sacred thrives on it.

The Latin word profane literally means *pro,* "outside", and *fanum,* "temple". The sacred and the profane are separated into two distinct arenas. Foremost, the sacred protects its own exclusive area of control from which the profane is excluded. This **exclusion** is the essential characteristic of the profane. Hence the profane is described as the **other** reality. It is a vague and common reality outside the realm of the sacred in sharp contrast to its compelling and powerful identity.

In the Old Testament narratives the word profane shares some similarities with the Latin etymology. Its most frequent use is in the verbs "to defile" and "to pollute". It is also used to imply the opposite of holy, as "ritually unclean" or "impure". However, the profane is generally translated into **common,** especially in connection to being "apart" from the holy. To profane something holy is to make it common, ordinary, in stark opposition to the uniqueness of the holy. As the following examples show:

Ez. 42:20 It had a wall around it, five hundred cubits long and five hundred cubits broad, to make a **separation** between the **holy** and the **common.**

Ez. 44:23 . . . and show them how to distinguish between the **unclean** and the **clean.**

The Gospels depict Jesus as abiding by the law, but sometimes he is also portrayed as challenging the law. Although he may appear at times to transgress the commandments, he does not condemn them. He does, however, castigate the hypocrisy of the priests that

---

[25] The holy is at all times in danger of being misrepresented. The origin of the holy, as we have said, is Yahweh, not the persons, the places or the objects upon which is conferred a sacred quality. The nuance is important since it is Yahweh's promise that is eternal while his prophets are mortal.

regulate the law. Foremost, Jesus is depicted as the prototype who inaugurates a new law.

His new rule supplants all other commandments: he says to **love** your God above anything else, but also to love your neighbor as yourself. The emphasis of the message is not the opposition between one God and other gods, but love. Jesus transcends the dichotomy between the holy and the common, yet he does not dull the distinction between the two. In fact, he inaugurates a new kingdom; ie, Christianity.

> Mt. 22:21 "Render therefore to Caesar the things that are Caesar's, and to God the things that are God's."

Jesus reverses the order of worldly things. What was profane is now sacred. He consecrates the common and makes it sacred, while he denounces the sacred hierarchies of the worldly powers.

the sacred	vs	*the profane*
the kingdom of God	vs	this world
the impure	vs	the priests
the unclean	vs	the zealous

Jesus' realm is outside the reach of the worldly powers. His kingdom, however, is not inaugurated to overthrow the worldly system, since it is based on the power of love. His kingdom is not of this world either, but from a world yet to be created by faith and **solidarity** between the believers. It is a place for those who forsake their share of this world for a part in the other.

As he explains to his disciples, only those who understand the **language** of the **parables** have access to his kingdom. And Jesus is the **door** to another realm of meaning: from the **physical** to the **spiritual,** and from the **literal** to the **metaphorical.** In essence, the parable is nothing else than an allegorical story, which is nothing more than an extended metaphor.[26] In the quote below, Jesus explains the meaning of such parables to his disciples, who themselves cannot yet understand.

> Mt. 13:10 Then the disciples came and said to him, "Why do you speak to them in **parables?**" And he answered them, "To

---

[26] As the Dictionary of the French Academy explains, the allegory is nothing else than an extended metaphor: "La parabole est en quelque sorte une autre forme de l'allégorie et l'allégorie est une figure qui n'est autre chose qu'une métaphore prolongée" Dictionnaire de l'Académie, Paris, Hachette, 1932.

142

you it has been given to **know the secrets of the kingdom of heaven,** but to them it has not been given. For to him who has will more be given, and he will have abundance; but from him who has not, even what he has will be taken away. This is why I speak to them in parables, **because seeing they do not see, and hearing they do not hear, nor do they understand.**"[27]

Jesus takes great care to point out that the **key** to his message will be lost by those caught up in the material aspect of the worldly existence. In the same manner as the true meaning of the message from the miracles is lost to the marvel and spectacle of the **sign.** The world would soon rather forget that Jesus cures the unclean, the outcasts and the excluded which society abhors and segregates. His miracles transgress the boundaries of the sacred and transcend them. By doing so, he shatters the structure of the sacred and the hierarchy on which society is built.

There is more to the profane than one might expect, even though the sacred consolidates all the attention on itself and dismisses the profane as a non-entity, as something remote and insignificant. We have seen that the profane is repudiated as the common, the ordinary, the hidden; it is decried as the **other.** And as such it is kept apart from the sacred hierarchy. The sacred tries to keep this **other** reality **overshadowed** and hidden so as to highlight its own power and play down the reality of the profane. As we have seen in Genesis, the serpent is a symbol of the Goddess and the tree is a metaphor of Asherah. These religious truths have been deliberately excluded from the divine reality of the Old Testament. These examples represent the profane and excluded reality in the religious experience.

Even though the sacred deliberately tries to deprecate the profane, it is nonetheless a reality, a dynamic entity essential to the existence and the survival of the sacred experience.

As Jesus focuses on the profane reality of the poor, the sick, the prostitutes, the possessed, the foreigners, the Gentiles and the slaves, he points to a reality that is excluded from the Jewish religious world dominated by the priestly order. In spite of the religious authority of the priests, he elected the outcasts as the beneficiaries of his kingdom. He reveals that the **other** reality is the essence of his message of love which exposes the true purpose of religion. As a result, he broke the foundation of the old precepts of the religious

---

[27] Also, Mk. 4:1-20; Lk. 8:10-15.

structure and activated a new reality that transcends the old religious order.[28]

Yet the profane has a specific function in the realm of the religious: it is an adumbrated and hidden quality that symbolizes the unacknowledged side of reality.

Lk. 1:35 "The Holy Spirit will come upon you, and the **power** of the Most High will **overshadow** you; therefore the child to be born will be called holy, the **Son of God**."

Here, Mary's identity is **overshadowed** from the holy. Her role has been kept in the background so that Jesus can accomplish his mission. We have also seen how the segregation is characteristic of the profane; as the hidden, the other and the excluded reality. Mary, first as a mother and then as a woman, is excluded from the symbolic triad of procreation; eg, the Father, the Son, and the Holy Spirit.

Even though the Holy Spirit is the only "person" that does not have a gender connotation, it does have numerous feminine attributes; ie, "life-giving Love", "the giver of life", and "breath".[29] In contrast to the affiliation of the Father and the Son, the identity of the Holy Spirit is, to say the least, **overshadowed.** Nevertheless, behind it lies the mystery of an-**other** hidden spiritual vitality.

The Holy Spirit is a profane reality of the Mother.

Among the numerous metaphors used to describe the Holy Spirit, many have several things in common; ie, "genesis", "breath", "dove", and "the giver of life". All point to a feminine origin of the principle of life.

---

[28] Segregation is an integral part of the system on which society is built. It appears to be a vital part of it. Society lives by the dynamic interaction between the integrated structure and the outcasts. Apparently, the survival of society is based on the outcasts as scapegoats. In other words, the sacred opposes the threat from the outer reality—the profane—which it does not understand and fears. See Michel Foucault, Madness and Civilization, New York, Pantheon Books, 1965.

[29] The appellation of "life-giving Love" is taken from the Encyclical, *Divinum Illud Munus,* by Pope Leo XIII on the Holy Spirit, May 9th, 1897. While "the giver of life" is taken from the Encyclical Letter, *Dominum et Vivificantem,* by Pope John Paul II, on the Holy Spirit as well, given the day of the Pentecost May 18th, 1986.

the physical	*the metaphysical*
pro**creation**	creation in Genesis
father v mother	God v man
child	woman
	in the New Testament
	Father v Son
	Holy Spirit

Most of all, the profane reality of the Goddess has been excluded from the creation—and **pro**creation—myths of Genesis. She has been vilified as an idol and opposed by Yahweh. It turns out that Asherah was a scapegoat, denounced and discredited as idolatry.[30]

The wholly other

Emile Durkheim first introduced the dichotomy between sacred and profane in his book on "primitive" religion.[31] Several years later, a landmark work on the "holy" was published. It was written by Rudolf Otto.[32] Unlike the sociological method of Durkheim, Otto was more preoccupied with the "feeling" aspect rather than the "rational" expression of the holy which he labeled the "numinous". It is in this work that he first introduced the expression "wholly other".[33]

Otto developed the concept because he perceived a need to expand the inventory of "expressions" to better describe the *mysterium* aspect of the holy. As he would explain: ". . . something of whose character we can *feel,* without being able to give it clear conceptual expression."[34] Concepts like "supernatural" and "transcendent" were usually used to define such a unique quality of the "numinous".

As we will see, this concept is not only useful but indispensable.

---

[30] This is true for most religions, since belief is amplifed by the dynamic opposition to other cults. For more insight about the opposition of the sacred and the profane see Roger Caillois, L'Homme et le Sacré, Paris, Gallimard, 1939, and, Mircea Eliade, The Sacred and the Profane, New York, Harper & Row, 1959, and, Cosmos and History, New York, Harper & Row, 1959.

[31] Emile Durkheim, The Elementary Forms of the Religious Life, New York, Free Press, 1965.

[32] Rudolf Otto, The Idea of the Holy, London, Oxford University Press, 1923.

[33] Ibid. 25-30.

[34] Ibid. 30.

It helps to fully understand the whole religious experience. It becomes essential to show the **whole** interrelation and the transcendental link between the sacred and the profane into the wholly other.

Otto did not develop his idea of the **wholly other** as a logical result of the dynamics between the sacred and the profane. He defined the **wholly other** as what stands beyond the realm of the intelligible. The sphere where the divine manifests itself, namely, the unfathomable and the ineffable. First, the unfathomable suggests that one is unable to understand and express his feelings of **awe** in the face of the holy. Second, the ineffable implies that words are inadequate to explain such an experience. Better still, no **known** language is able to fully disclose the *mysterium*.

Unlike Otto, we are not so much concerned with the **feeling** as with the expressions of the holy as related by the narratives. We are less concerned with what Moses felt at the sight of the burning bush, than how the writers/editor have related the experience. The Holy Bible is full of accounts of such **mysterious** experiences. Consequently, it is possible to explore the symbolic nature of that experience through the account. In other words, the text is the data that allows us to analyze the holy systematically.[35]

●

Etymologically, the adverb wholly has two meanings. The first, an older sense derived from ''whole'', means in its **entirety,** in full, the sum total, all of it: hence, **inclusively.** The second sense is implied by the word **entirely,** as to suggest the exclusion of others, solely: hence, **exclusively.** The terminology may appear ambiguous at the outset, but it will become clearer as we go along. And, as we will see, it is rather insightful. The equivocalness of **wholly** fits exactly into the essence of the **two-ness** or **twofold-ness** of the sacred and the profane. Adding the word **other** to **wholly** we further expand the scope of its meaning.

> >**wholly other;** the dynamic **center** that is exclusively **other** because words cannot express that otherness: the **sacred,** the *mysterium,* the **ineffable.** The mystery of the holy is always other than the expressions that try to describe it. The **exclusively other** can be seen as the center represent-

---

[35] I first began to develop the idea about the wholly other in my Masters thesis entitled: l'Interprétation Religieuse de l'Origine Mythique de la Nationalité: l'Inauguration de Monuments Nationaux (1840-1940), Montréal, Bibliothèque de l' UQAM, 1978.

ed by Yahweh—the **holy**—who **set** his prophets, his priests and his people **apart** from the **other** people.

<**wholly other;** the **whole** and the dynamic reality that is beyond the center and beyond the hierarchy of the sacred. It is the yet **unknown,** the yet **undiscovered,** the **unfathomable;** ie, the other religions, the other cultures, the mystery of the universe and eternity: the **inclusively other.** Beyond its center is the hidden reality of the goddess Asherah—the tree. And beyond the periphery of the chosen people stands the whole reality of the other gods and other cultures.

Only when the sacred opens up to and includes the profane does it ascend to the **wholly other.** Only when the profane becomes part of the sacred does it ascend to the **wholly other.**

In Exodus, the words of Yahweh preempt the sign of the burning bush as the source of the holy. It is Yahweh's **words** that are at the **center** and from which he reveals his **will.** Yet Yahweh's identity— image—remains obscure and exclusively other.

Whereas the **profane** reality and space are excluded from the holy, God separates the Holy ground from the profane, from the common. This realm of the **other** is the reality of the profane, comprised of such examples as the other gods/goddesses, the other religions that make up the **whole** religious reality of the world.

In the Gospels, the transfiguration reveals Jesus Christ at the center with God: "his face shone like the sun". Again, God reveals his "beloved Son" to the world through his spoken Word.[36] Here too, the voice of God comes from nowhere. The Word of God reveals that God is with us and that Jesus Christ, as his Son, is himself God and as such he shares a place at the center.[37] This time, Jesus Christ's identity is fully disclosed by his own physical "body".

Jesus Christ as the Son of God is himself holy, but as the son of Mary he partakes in the profane reality of the human condition. Jesus' twofold origin—that of God and "man"—embodies the whole spectrum of the religious reality and the two poles of a true spirituality: the sacred and the profane. This twofold unity transcends the exclusive holiness of God and reaches beyond the boundaries of his divine essence through his human nature and into the

---

[36] Mt. 17:1-8, Mk. 9:1-8; Lk. 9:28-36.

[37] At Jesus' baptism, God speaks through the heavens while the Holy Spirit is revealed by the dove descending on Christ, testifying to the reality of the three persons of the Trinity. Mt. 3:13-17; Mk. 1:9-11; Lk. 3:21-22; Jn. 1:32-34.

wholly other. Jesus Christ, as the **wholly other,** transcends the exclusivity of the holy into the inclusively whole divine reality. The wholly other is both center and totality, one single reality.

Jesus/man-Christ/God

Hence, the profane reality becomes as important as the sacred in the religious experience. Only then can the dynamic interrelation between the sacred and the profane become alive in the **wholly other** and transcend the two spiritual entities into **one** whole dynamic reality of being.

•

Christ, as God, is the mysterious holy center from which everything originates and everything flows. As God he is the center of power, as "man" Jesus is the **door** to that power, the hope of the powerless. The Gospels dispel the notion that the profane reality of the impure and unclean should be excluded. It recounts that it should be embraced instead. Jesus dissipates the barriers and highlights what is at the heart of faith: the **wholly other.** He denounces the segregation of the powerful and their institutions. He reaches out to the forgotten and the segregated by society: the sick, the poor, the possessed, the foreigners, the women, the Gentiles, the sinners the slaves.

Jesus inaugurates a law, that of **love.** Love as the total openness that blurs the boundaries between the sacred and the profane into the realm of the wholly other. His new command undoes the boundaries imposed by the sacred institutions. It exceeds the borders of the sacred and overflows into the profane world. The holy is no longer an **exclusive** arena accessible only to a limited few of the higher hierarchy. What was out of reach becomes accessible to all who believe. With love one can bypass the sacred institutions and have access to God. The power of Jesus' being opens the **door** to the wholly other realm.

Jesus Christ talked of two worlds. One that he identified with Caesar and the other with God. The two kingdoms, however, do not oppose each other in a political fashion.[38] The kingdom of God that Jesus speaks about is not of this world. It is a place where the faith in the Word creates a "world" onto itself, outside the boundaries of time and space. Faith in the message of the Word is the key to the creation of the kingdom of heaven.

---

[38] One might think of the "quasi-religion" typified by Marxism where the sterile antagonism of working class and ruling class just replaces one dictatorship by another.

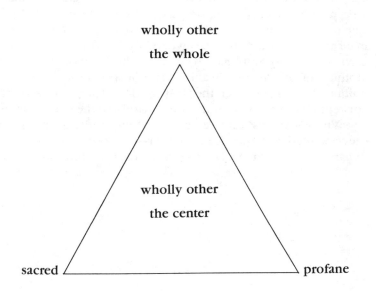

wholly other

the whole

wholly other

the center

sacred

profane

To conclude, the sacred triad and the Holy Trinity share some fundamental principles which can be illustrated as follows:

God the Father . . . . the holy/the center
Jesus Christ . . . . the wholly other/the whole
the Holy Spirit . . . . the profane/the overshadowed

As outlined earlier, the Holy Spirit has no gender status, yet it is called "the giver of life". Furthermore, the third person over-shadows Mary's identity. As such, the Holy Spirit conceals an-**other** reality, that of the profane reality of the Mother of God.

Lk. 1:35 The Holy Spirit will come upon you, and the power of the Most High will **overshadow** you; Therefore the child to be born will be called holy, the Son of God.

The narrative describes that the **power** of the "Most High" overshadows Mary as the Mother of Jesus, and as a woman. As we have said, it is in the nature of the sacred to "overshadow" and exclude the profane. Similar in fashion to the exclusion of the God-dess in Genesis. We have also seen how the metaphors and attributes associated with Mary are closely associated with the Holy Spirit. The most prominent of which are related to life and procreation in terms of "breath" and "the giver of life". Furthermore, the epithets of the Holy Spirit as "the giver of life", and of Mary, as the Mother of God, are closely akin.[39] The Gospels describe how the unique collusion between the Holy Spirit and Mary results in the conception of Jesus Christ, the Son of God and the Son of "man".

What the **overshadowed** reality of the Trinity unveils is that the metaphysical reality of the mother—and the woman—plays a dynamic, if not primordial, role in the creation of the world.[40]

---

[39] The reference to "the giver of life", in connection with Mary, is taken from the definition of the Dogma of the Assumption of Mary, by Pius XII, 11-12. See also Yves Congar, I Believe In The Holy Spirit, v. 1, New York, The Seabury Press, 1983, 163.

[40] Catholics have always been loyal devotees of Mary. In many instances she usually plays a role occupied by the **Paraclete.** They attribute to her the titles and functions of **comforter, advocate,** the defender of the believers. But mostly she is worshipped as the Mother of God; the kind and gentle intercessor, the giver of life. Yves Congar states that "There is a deep relationship between Mary, the mother of God, and the Holy Spirit". He further continues: "The part played in our upbringing by the Holy Spirit is that of **mother**—a mother who enables us to know our Father, God, and our brother, Jesus . . . the Holy Spirit has often been replaced in recent Catholic devotion by the Virgin Mary." He also points out the close link between the motherhood in God and the femininity of the Holy Spirit. See Yves Congar, I Believe in the Holy Spirit, New York, Seabury Press, 1983, vol. 1, 164, and vol. 3, 154-155.

PART THREE

NEW WORLD PERSPECTIVE: The American Frontier

Ever-returning Spring, Trinity sure to me you bring. . .

Walt Whitman
from ''The Threnody on the Death of Lincoln''

CHAPTER NINE

ZUNI: A Native's Cosmological View of the "World"

Why a chapter on the Zuni Pueblo? There are several reasons. First, because it allows us to display their splendid mythology. In many respects, the Zuni represent a beautiful example of the aboriginal cultures that thrived in North America. And as the title of the third part of this book implies, it allows us to disclose the Zuni's conception of the "world" which was inaugurated long before the so-called "civilized world" made its imprint on the whole continent.

Secondly, the Zuni Pueblo exemplifies the natives' struggle for survival against the onslaught of colonization which began several centuries ago by predominantly Christian settlers. What remains of the aboriginal cultures today shows how detrimental immigration was to these cultures. Ironically, a great part of the pilgrims that came to the New World had fled injustices and religious persecutions in their own countries. They nevertheless came armed with the belief in the superiority of their predominantly Judeo-Christian precepts, which they finally managed to impose on North America as a whole. The faith in their divine cause justified their fight against the aboriginal people who had lived on these lands for centuries. The Zuni, like many other "Indians", were labeled by the new immigrants as the "heathen", the "savages", and the "pagans". As a result, they were categorized as the **profane** reality; ie, the **adversary** who had to be decimated. Fortunately, the Zuni managed to survive.

Thirdly, the metaphorical aspect of Zuni language is at the core of its cosmology. In their rituals and their everyday life the Zuni use numerous metaphors to depict how "everything" is related to the "same thing". **Language** is a dynamic principle of the whole Zuni mentality.

Finally, among the many native cultures of North America the Zuni still live by the "word" of a compelling cosmology. Their self-enclosed **cosmos** is a typical example of what Emile Durkheim calls "sociocentrism".[1] The composition and arrangement of their collective order is typical of many other native cultures. But what is particular to Zuni mythology is some analogies it shares with the creation myths of Genesis. While the Bible describes the creation of the world in terms of time; namely, **seven** days, the Zuni relate the creation of the world in terms of space; namely, **seven** orientations. In Genesis the seventh day is sacred. For the Zuni the seventh space is also sacred. The etymology of the Hebrew word "to swear", for instance, literally means "to seventh oneself".[2] In Zuni mythology the seventh space is referred to as the sacred **"Center"**: it is described as the Middle Place, and the Middle Time. Similarly, in the Bible the tree that lies in the "midst" of the garden is a metaphor of the Goddess. In Zuni Mythology the center is a metaphor of the Earth Mother.

•

Zuni is the name of the people; eg, Pueblo. It is also the name of their small village located on the Indian Reservation in the McKinley county of New Mexico.[3] Zuni is situated thirty miles south of Gallup, and about the same distance west of the Continental Divide.

The Zuni Pueblo are noted for their skills in making silver and turquoise jewelry. They are also famous for the ceremonial dance of the Shalako.[4]

---

[1] "It has quite often been said that **man** began to conceive things by relating them to himself. The above allows us to see more precisely what this anthropocentrism, which might better be called *sociocentrism,* consists of. The center of the first schemes of nature is not the **individual;** it is society. It is this that is objectified, not man . . . It is by virtue of the same mental disposition that so many peoples have placed the center of the world, "the navel of the earth", in their own political or religious capital, ie, at the place which is the center of their moral life. Similarly, but in another order of ideas, the creative force of the universe and everything in it was first conceived as a mythical ancestor, the generator of the society." From Emile Durkheim & Marcel Mauss, Primitive Classification, Chicago, University of Chicago Press, 1963, 86-87.

[2] See Gen. 21:31. Originally, the Sabbath was apparently related to the Babylonian day of moon cult called *shabattu*. See Max Weber, Ancient Judaism, New York, The Free Press, 1952, 149.

[3] In February 1988 the population was 8299. Data from the Zuni Area Chamber of Commerce 1989.

[4] Gregory C. Crampton, The Zunis of Cibola, Salt Lake City, University of Utah Press, 1977, 56.

The Pueblo lies in a small valley of the Zuni River which takes its source from the Little Colorado. It is one of the oldest farming communities in the United States. They are the descendants of the people of the "Seven Cities" of Cibola. They were given that name by a Spanish expedition led by the Franciscan Friar Marcos de Niza in 1539. His embellished accounts of the Seven Cities of Gold lured another expedition led by Francisco Vasquez de Coronado the next year. The first expedition of the Spaniards apparently mistook the golden reflection of the mica, the material that the Pueblo used to cover their windows, for the precious metal.

The Spaniards didn't find any gold, but nevertheless they tried to impose their rule until 1680. At that time a Pueblo revolt tentatively liberated them from the colonial rule. Since, they have earned a reputation for being a fiercely independent people, deeply religious, loyal to their traditions, and proud to speak their language. This is one reason why the Zuni survived through the centuries despite the attempts made by the missionaries to convert them.[5] Of the seven cities that the Spaniards discovered in the sixteenth century, only Zuni remains today. The village, as seen today, bears the marks of acculturation.

Zuni cosmology is closely akin to its environment. Their whole culture reflects the beauty of nature that is all around them. Like many other native people of the continent, the symbolic representations of their fauna and flora are omnipresent in all their art and rituals. What makes Zuni cosmology particularly noteworthy though, is their semantic description of space. The movement of the sun, the moon, and the stars, altogether with changes in the winter and summer solstices, have inspired a "dynamic" conception of the world.

The beauty of the surrounding landscape is overwhelmingly present in all of their artistic endeavors. Not surprisingly, Zuni cosmology reveals that "the beautiful is dynamic".[6] This dynamism is also revealed in their lore and in every other aspect of their collective life. Everything in their social arrangement reflects the aesthetic and kinetic aspect of nature. Zuni cultural life is in effect a

---

[5] "The Zuni faith, as revealed in this sketch of more than three hundred and fifty years of Spanish intercourse, is as a drop of oil in water, surrounded and touched at every point, yet in no place penetrated or changed inwardly by the flood of alien belief that descended upon it." Frank Hamilton Cushing, from Zuni, Selected Writings of Frank Hamilton Cushing, edited, with an introduction by Jesse Green, Lincoln, University of Nebraska Press, 1979, 181.

[6] Barbara Tedlock, The Beautiful and the Dangerous: Zuni Ritual and Cosmology as an Aesthetic, in Conjunctions: Bi-Annual Volumes of New Writing no. 6, New York, MacMillan Publishing Co., 1984.

metaphor of the "dynamic" in nature, and everything is symbolically arranged in its image. Their art, their elaborate rituals, their dances and their pantomimes, everything is a **mimetic** expression of their perception of the cosmos as one and "the same thing".

Zuni society is based on a system of symbolic classifications described by Frank Hamilton Cushing as "mytho-sociologic".[7] Zuni mythology and cosmology are so closely intertwined with their social and religious order that they are in effect the "same thing".

Social life was originally divided into regions according to a "four-cornered world".[8] The number and orientations of these spaces reflect the basic composition of their cosmological perception of the world. All the members of the Zuni Pueblo belong to one or the other of these respective regions. The divisions involved all of the Seven Cities of Cibola. These areas are systematically parted into clans, which are split into totems depicted as animals. These totems are then separated into parts or attributes of the animal. Each member of the Pueblo belongs to a clan, and each member of the clan assumes the name of the part or attribute of the totem. Through this intricate classification, which they believe is made according to the "mirror" image of nature, each Zuni participates in the cosmological and social life of the Pueblo.

Zuni society is matrilineal and matrilocal. The mother's household is the basic social unit. The children have to marry outside their parents' clans and when they marry they live in the household of the bride's mother. This pattern was the traditional norm.[9]

What impressed the Spaniards during their first expedition to the "Seven Cities" was the architecture of the villages: the multistory dwellings were harmoniously built one on top of the other. The only access was an opening on the roof accessible through a ladder that leaned against the outside wall.

Although invisible to the visitor, these villages were divided into several orientations. These partitions have an important significance to the inhabitants since they position each member in relation to the whole community. Each quarter is placed according to a spatial direction. They reflect the four fundamental orientations of the sunrise and sunset of the summer and winter solstices: namely, the north-east to the north-west, and, the south-east to the south-west.

---

[7] Frank Hamilton Cushing, Ibid. 185-193.

[8] Barbara Tedlock, Zuni and Quiche dream sharing and interpreting, Dreaming, ed. by Barbara Tedlock, Cambridge, Cambridge University Press, 1987, 107.

[9] This custom is not strictly applied anymore.

In addition, two other orientations complete the foursome order of the world: the zenith—the above—and the nadir—the below. The whole cosmic reality is finally rounded out by the seventh point described as the "Middle". The "Center", for the Zuni, acts as a synthetic metaphor for all the orientations.

This classification is meant to reflect the dynamic movement of the planets in harmony with the Zuni's whole cosmological perception of life. This kinetic movement of the planets inspired the concept of "directionality". The four orientations represent the daily movement of the sun in concert with its seasonal change on its axis during the winter and summer solstices. In addition, the zenith and the nadir become a six-fold "directionality", and finally with the seventh point at its center, the whole arrangement inspires a dynamic multi-dimensional quality of space.[10]

The beautiful and the dangerous

Zuni mythology does not escape the dichotomy between the sacred and the profane that we have talked about in previous chapters. These two principles are categorized as the "beautiful" and the "dangerous".[11] Their interaction reflects an aesthetic and dynamic vision of nature, and numerous metaphors are used to portray the "balance" of nature:

the sacred	vs	*the profane*
the beautiful	vs	the dangerous
the dynamic	vs	the dull
the colorful	vs	the dark
the clear	vs	the indistinct
the multi	vs	the plain

The duality is also expressed in terms of time and space:

morning	vs	evening
summer	vs	winter
above	vs	below

Furthermore, according to Zuni beliefs, there are two types of beings:

the cooked	vs	the raw

---

[10] Jane Young, Signs From the Ancestors, Albuquerque, University of New Mexico Press, 1988. For more insight about the Zuni cosmology see Ms. Young's book.

[11] Barbara Tedlock, Ibid.

The cooked—or ripe—are called the "daylight beings" because they live on cooked food and live under the special protection of the Sun Father. The second group of beings rely on the raw food as well as the cooked food prepared by the daylight people. The daylight people are also split into:

the valuable   vs   the poor

Women are valuable by virtue of their gender, whereas men have no value until they are initiated into the religious Kachina Society. To the Zuni, "poor" literally means "without religion".[12]

The Water Skate

The number "four" is a key number in Zuni mythology. It is central to the origin and foundation of Zuni. According to their creation myths, the first people travelled through the darkness of the **four** underworlds before they reached the surface of our present world. At that time, they were blinded by the light of the sun. They spent four time periods—four days or four years, depending on the version—searching for the **Center.** The "Center Place" was finally found when the Water Skate, with the magical powers given to him by the Sun Father, stretched out its "four" legs, one on each of the "four" directions of the sunrise and sunset of both the summer and winter solstices. The place where he rested his heart and navel marked the "Center Place". This point also identifies the heart and navel of **Earth Mother.**[13] The "Center" revealed by the Water Skate is the site on which the Zuni village is built.

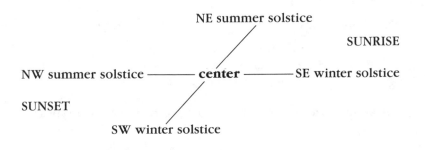

[12] See Barbara Tedlock, Zuni and Quiche Dream Sharing and Interpreting, in, Dreaming, ed. by Barbara Tedlock, Cambridge, Cambridge University Press, 1987, 108-109.

[13] It is interesting to note that the Zuni word for Earth Mother— *'awitelin tsitta*—has the same root as the word "four"— *'a:witen'*—. Jane Young, Ibid. 99.

The numerical sequence of number "four" becomes, with the extension of the zenith and the nadir, number "six". The number "six" with the addition of the "Middle" finally adds up to the **sacred** number "seven". The arrangement completes the spherical balance and dynamic "directionality".

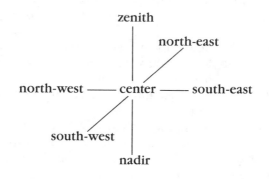

All six orientations are centered around the "Middle" place where Zuni is built. Yet under the center of the village itself is another center. In the fourth underground, in the house of the chief priest, below the altar, lies a heart-shaped rock, which is described as "the heart of the world". Its arteries reach out toward the same four directions as did the Water Skate when he stretched his four legs to find the "Center".

The significance of the "center" remains in effect equivocal. More specifically, polyonymous, since the "Center" has many different names. It is simultaneously the "middle", the "center", the heart, the navel of the Water Skate, and the center of Zuni and the world. The "middle" is all these things because, as the Zuni say, they are all "the same thing".[14] This way of thinking is quite characteristic of the Zuni. The words describe different things, yet they are all—related to—"the same thing".

At the beginning of the "world" there were both the spatial "center" and the temporal "center": the "Middle Place" and the "Middle Time". They may appear as two different concepts, but to the Zuni they are "the same thing". Accordingly, the Zuni name for the village is *'itiwana,* which means "Center" but also "winter solstice". The first is the "Center" in space, while the second is the "Center" in time. Therefore, all the symbols that relate to their

---

[14] Jane Young, Ibid. 106.

cosmological "world" are a succession, a repetition, and a substitution of metaphors into a whole "dynamic asymmetry" that reveals—or relates—that everything is "the same thing".[15]

This polyonymous aspect of Zuni symbolism is best depicted by the dynamic relation between the **beautiful** and the **dangerous.** The beautiful is described as having a "multi" quality as opposed to the plain and indistinct aspect of the dangerous. The beautiful is multilayered, multicolored, multitextured, multisensory, and multilingual.

Although the tautology of Zuni language may appear redundant at first, a closer look reveals that the repetition suggests the idea of relatedness. It is not the expressions by themselves that are meaningful, but rather the connection between them in relation to the whole cosmological outlook.

Zuni ritual life is filled with this "multi" aspect of meaning. This aspect of their culture is equally applied in their profane arena. The Zuni Tribal Fair, for instance, which is considered a mundane activity, is organized in the same manner. The symbolic representations of sacred places, objects, sounds and colors, repeated incessantly during the dance, become a meaningful repetition that links each symbolic part together in one cosmic being, as "the same thing". The symbols are parts that are related to the whole order of things.[16]

To the Zuni, the sun and the moon are "living beings". As such, they play a significant role as they move across the sacred space. Some of their rituals and dances duplicate the planetary movement. Every single aspect of the environment is described as a living being. Both the "outer" and "inner" spaces are fused together into the sacred ritual. Celestial objects are not seen as external but as active participants in the ceremonial. The cosmos is perceived as one whole intertwined entity. Accordingly, the whole array of symbolic representations operates in connection with the principles of "continuity" and "similarity", based on the idea of unity and balance of all life. To the Zuni, the whole "world" is a dynamic "being" with a "multi" facet quality.

The Zuni's conception of time shares the polyonymous principles also. The "world" was created in the "beginning" of time,

---

[15] Barbara Tedlock, The Beautiful and Dangerous, Ibid. 259.

[16] When Zuni people pray, they ask for "more"; namely, more rain for their crops. All is related to the concern that the Sun Father continues his daily journey and that the rain falls in abundance. The sun's light coupled with water and Earth Mother are the essence of all life. "More" is also related to the idea of "everything" associated with the desire for the accumulation of things and prosperity. The Zuni pray for more success in hunting, many children and a long life, as well as an increase in jewelry sales.

and the beginning is re-enacted, re-created, and re-lived in the ritual. Past, present, and future coexist. There is no temporal separation between the time of creation and the here and now of the ritual. It accounts for the symbolic "presentness" of Zuni cosmological life represented in the *'itiwana,* the "Center", the here and now of "time" and "space". The creation of the world in the past is transcended into the present and in the future by following the ways of the ancestors.

•

The Zuni Pueblo is a good illustration of the "cosmos" as a self-enclosed, self-sufficient social and cultural reality, comparable in many ways to the religious reality of Israel. In a similar fashion, the word "Zuni" stands for the people, the village, the language, the religion, the mythology, the economy, and the social organization.

Yet this sacred "cosmos", as typified here by the Zuni, has been categorized by the settlers as a **profane** reality. A reality that was an obstacle to the development of the New World. As such, the natives were viewed as the "adversaries" to the colonization of the "promised land" and were **excluded** from the mythological founding of the nation.

THE MYTHICAL QUEST FOR INDEPENDENCE:
A People's Search for Identity

When I switched my major from economics to theology at Loyola College in the fall of 1970, the province of Quebec was in the midst of a political turmoil. During what is now known as the October Crisis, British Trade Commissioner James Cross and Quebec Labor Minister Pierre Laporte were both kidnapped by the *Front de Libération du Québec* (F.L.Q.). James Cross was later released, but Pierre Laporte was found strangled in the trunk of an abandoned car on the eastern outskirts of Montreal. The "Crisis" triggered the adoption by the Liberal Government of Canada of the War Measures Act and the army was sent into the province.

The circumstances that led to this dramatic turn of events could be traced back to the British invasion of a small but growing French colony of *Nouvelle-France* in 1760. The "Conquest" was to be the beginning of a people's ongoing **struggle** for survival.

In order to maintain peace in the newly conquered colony, the English undertook a policy of *laissez faire* toward the Catholic Church. As the new spiritual leader, the Church promoted in the minds of the people a "distinct" vision of its own identity and destiny. Looking back, hardly any political party could have inspired such a collective will to overcome the unforeseeable obstacles of history.

From the time I first left Italy to immigrate to Montreal, in 1956, I witnessed enormous changes in the "people" of Quebec. The

Catholic Church was omnipresent when we first arrived, and had been for at least three centuries. All aspects of "French Canadian" life was imprinted with the Church's authority.

In the early nineteen-sixties, two major events were to change the Church's hold over the people: Vatican II in Rome, and the emergence of the Quiet Revolution—*la Révolution Tranquille*—in Quebec. In a matter of years, the Church's power rapidly eroded. In less than a decade, the priests and nuns who dominated schools and hospitals were replaced by lay people. The Church was losing an increasing number of its believers. Those who lost their "faith" embraced the growing nationalist fervor. And as the *québécois* progressively abandoned the Church, they joined the ranks of the emerging political **quest** for independence.

It is this "quest" that is the subject of this chapter. We will try to explain how a desire for spiritual salvation was transformed into a movement for political liberation. As Claude Lévi-Strauss observed, nothing in today's society is more mythical than political ideology. He wrote:

> But what gives the myth an operational value is that the specific pattern described is timeless; it explains the present and the past as well as the future. This can be made clear through a comparison between myth and what appears to have largely replaced it in modern societies, namely, politics.[1]

This "quest" for independence focussed on a message of mythical proportions.

•

Ironically, myth and history appear today as conflicting in meaning as in function. They are both stories, yes, but each relates to different aspects of events that are recounted. Both are equally considered to be true stories by those who relate their content. Yet myth is primarily concerned with accounts of the origins taking place in a primordial time, a so called **time** beyond the realm of history. History, on the other hand, is a chronological compendium of historical data.

One can best differentiate myth from history as two distinct forms of language. Foremost, history is the realm of the historian and his work, whereas myth reaches out to all men, women, and children regardless of class, position, and age. All are captivated by

---

[1] Claude Lévi-Strauss, Structural Anthropology, New York, Basic Books Inc., 1963, 209.

myth. Everybody is enchanted by the mythical stories, fairy tales, and legends that have been generated by different cultures.

Myth is concise, symbolic, meaningful, and efficient. Its stories relate to events and heroes beyond the ordinary human sphere. These stories are concerned with god(s), super-heroes, and heroic deeds. What separates myth from history is its description of a special **class** of beings and their activities. They deal mostly with the powers that rule the world: wherein God or the gods are metaphors for the unfathomable powers—as yet inconceivable hierarchies—that rule the world. For the most part, these stories have an enduring quality that reflects the intrinsic and significant aspects of a mentality derived from the different cultures they emerged from.

Myth relates how a new reality came into being, how a new "world" was created. It describes the actions of the super-heroes or the god(s) in their creative endeavor. Why are certain things forbidden? What legitimates a particular authority? Why does human misery exist? Why do people suffer and die? To sum it up, myth decodes the meaningful events of the world. These events evolved in a time beyond history; ie, *in illo tempore.*[2] Thus, this ethereal dimension in time and space is the primary gap that **separates** myth from history. It is the "fuzzy" boundary between history and myth.

History is foremost an exhaustive and detailed account of all significant events that occurred in the past. With the scientific application of historiography, history has been stripped of any mythical content. It was not the case of the history books of several decades ago. One look at older history books reveals how they were filled with heroic embellishment which have nothing to do with historical truth. The interpretation of the events surrounding General Custer's battle at Little Bighorn, for instance, has varied tremendously over time. Some of the earlier versions were, to say the least, mythical, and particularly unfavorable toward the "Indians".

The above comparison between myth and history is well illustrated in the example of the discovery of *Nouvelle-France* (New-France). According to Mircea Eliade, myth is essentially an account that describes the events that are at the origin of a **new** reality founded and created by civilizing heroes or god(s) in the beginning of time. The discovery of **New**-France, for example, has been inscribed in history as the legitimate origins of a "new" national reality. The new beginnings inaugurate the grounds of mythical significance. The "ancestral" **heroes** are the founders of a "new" national entity at the beginning of a new history. The founders' identities are cele-

---

[2] Mircea Eliade, Myth and Reality, New York, Harper & Row, 1963.

brated as heroic and are separated from the mass of historical events. In the U.S., for instance, Columbus day is a national holiday.[3] The national event celebrates the hero as the prototype of a new cultural and national reality. The pioneer is not so much famed as a person but as a **symbol** of a new cultural reality. As history shows, because of **Amerigo** Vespucci, the **New World** became known as **America** on maps as early as 1507.

Christopher Columbus *discovered* America in 1492

Jacques Cartier *discovered* New-France in 1594

These national heroes were the **first** to inaugurate a new historical and national reality. They were elevated above ordinary human beings and other historical characters. As a result, society will commemorate these super-heroes by erecting monuments in their honor. These monuments **consecrate** the significant part they played in the foundation and creation of a new national entity and identity.[4]

There is an inherent contradiction in the concept of the "discovery", however. How could the New World be discovered when it was already inhabited by native cultures? To validate the Christian "discovery", these natives had to be dismissed as having no cultural and moral value of their own. Being labeled as heathen and pagan justified their need for "civilization". Therefore, the "discovery" was strictly a European colonialist imposition upon the native cultures to justify the taking of the biggest piece of free real estate ever "discovered". Today, such historical value given to the discovery is debatable, since it is more mythical than anything else. But it shows how the mythical process is a propaganda tool for the justification of any form of colonialism and imperialism.

•

The chronicle of the origin of a new reality has an important mythological significance in history, yet the **struggle** for the nation's identity is also essential.[5]

---

[3] Although it was soon found out that Columbus did not find his way to India, the inhabitants he met on the continent are still referred to by the wrongful appellation of "Indians".

[4] My work on the inauguration of monuments shows that the fine line between historical figures and mythical heroes disappears at the dedication; L'Interprétation Religieuse de l'Origine Mythique de la Nationalité, Montréal, UQAM, 1978. More on the subject in the next chapter.

[5] The connection between nationalism and the principle of opposition was first proposed by Maurice Lemire, Les Grands Thèmes Nationalistes du Roman Historique Canadien-Français, Québec, PUQ, 1970.

sacred	vs	*profane*
the colonialists	vs	the natives
the Christians	vs	the pagans

The opposition establishes the sacredness of the colonial endeavor, especially in respect to the belief of the mission to "civilize" and to convert the savage heathen who represented an obstacle to the development of the new nation. We have already typified the Zuni as the heathen reality to be converted. As a profane reality, they were seen as an obstacle to the development of the New World.

Christian civilization	vs	the heathen
British civilization	vs	the pagan
French civilization	vs	the savage

New-France will evolve dramatically from the time of its foundation. Its historical discovery allowed the consecration of its origin as a legitimate nation regardless of the fate of the aboriginal cultures who lived in their ancestral lands.

•

The discovery of New-France that fills the first pages of history books of that nation was to be undermined by a tragic turn of events. In 1760, the colony was conquered by the British army and abandoned by France. In the process, the conquerors set their own political rules while recognizing the authority of the Catholic Church so as to appease the population.

The defeat and the abrupt change in the political allegiance left a deep scar in the collective memory of the French people. The result was to imprint ambivalent feelings of being a nation of colonized-colonialists, and to mark a **lord-victim** approach in regards to their history and their fate. The people were in political exile in their own land. The French, who were originally the Lords and colonialists in the New World, had become themselves the victims of colonialism imposed by the British. This turn of events will have enduring effects in the development of their destiny and history. It will set off the **beginning** of a peoples' **struggle** for survival.

The British conquest of New-France also reinstated the old rivalry between England and France and exported to North America the ancestral antagonism between Protestantism and Catholicism that had endured in Europe for several centuries.

The political struggle that emerged because of the conquest clearly outlined two distinct and rival cultural entities.

Abandoned by France, the people congregated under the leadership of the Catholic Church. From then on the French mentality would be shaped into a Catholic mold. With her new found authority the Church became preoccupied with the redemption of its people. The hierarchy promoted the principles of obedience to the Church as the only visible sign of salvation: *extra ecclesiam nulla salus;* ie, there is no salvation outside the Church. The Church encouraged students to shun the evils of business and commerce and to embrace liberal professions such as law, medicine, and the priesthood. The clerics preached to the population the benefits of agriculture as a privileged way of salvation. They urged women to marry young and have numerous children.

Meanwhile, by the end of the XVIIIth century, signs of the Industrial Revolution were visible all over England. The Kingdom was in a rapid transition from an agrarian to an industrial society. The roots of the cultural and economic development of capitalism had Protestant ethical overtones. Individual responsibility, freedom, industry, and success were believed to be visible signs of salvation. Max Weber described the ethic in terms of a **"secular asceticism".**[6] This **spirit** of capitalism would soon spread to all the British colonies of North America.

Suddenly, Canada became a battleground for two rival cultures, two languages, and two religions originating from two rival European colonial powers. On one hand, we have the French culture led by the Catholic Church whose authority lay in the hierarchy and in the assembly of believers as a visible sign of its invested power, described in terms of **collective asceticism.** This belief implied a faithful obedience to the principle of the Church as the only way toward salvation.

On the other hand, we have the English culture influenced by the Protestant ethic, described in terms of **secular asceticism.** The ethic favored individual initiative, industry (ie, hard work), responsibility, and financial success as a sign of election.

Hence, two cultures and two visions of the world inspired an antagonism that put the two collective entities against each other.

---

[6] Of course, when Max Weber talks about capitalism it is in terms of the "spirit" of capitalism, which implies an ethical and spiritual dimension to it. Not to be confused with the capitalistic anomalies of greed, speculation, and corruption we have witnessed in the 1980s. Max Weber, The Protestant Ethic and the Spirit of Capitalism, New York, Scribner, 1958.

Each was living in their **world** of sacred beliefs, opposing the other as a profane reality.

French Catholics	vs	English Protestants
collective asceticism	vs	secular asceticism
other-worldly	vs	this-worldly

•

Not until the first half of the XVIIIth century did the French-Canadian people begin to challenge the political rules set by the English and the Church.

During 1837-38, a movement emerged that began to question the authority of the Church and the political advantage of the English. A growing number of people from the French middle-class, as well as intellectuals, expressed their unhappiness with their share of political power. Louis-Joseph Papineau, the leader of the *Parti Canadien,* succeeded in rallying a majority of French people against the Catholic Church and the English. The nationalist outburst was brief. In 1838 the English crushed an armed insurrection and dispelled the leader and its followers.

As a result, the people were left in a political limbo. In time, the French-Canadians rallied back to the Church for guidance. The majority of the people who were tempted by the political solutions proposed by the nationalists returned to the Church's promise of collective salvation. Redemption would not be won through political means, but through obedience to the Church and through faith.

By the end of the XIXth century, the rapid changes brought by industrialization and urbanization began to undermine the Church's control over the faithful. Priests began to preach to people to have large families in order to overcome the English by number.[7] The policy of *la revenge des berceaux*—the revenge of the cradle—worked. As the population grew rapidly, people left the farm for the city. The cities were unable to handle the increasing number of people moving in. And because of the high level of urban unemployment a great deal of the people emigrated to the U.S. In order to limit the exodus, the Catholic hierarchy pioneered the development of agricultural lands in the northern parts of Quebec. These policies were devised to keep the people away from the evils of industrial cities controlled by the English. But despite the courage and endurance of the inhabitants, the harsh climate and poor economical benefits failed to keep the people on their farms.

---

[7] From a mere sixty thousand French-Canadians in 1760, their number grew to four million in 1980.

Urbanization was seen by the clerical elite as a threat to their authority. They had complete control over the farmer who lived in relative autonomy and isolation on his land. Not so for the people living in the cities who were being hired by the English industrialists and traders.

The rapid industrial development, which was out of the Church's control, was perceived as threatening the integrity of their flock. The economic power of the English was seen as an incursion in their clerical jurisdiction. Especially in light of the overwhelming presence of the Anglo-Saxon culture of Canada and the U.S.

Even though the French-Canadians renewed their allegiance to the Church in the years following the rebellious outburst, their vision of salvation underwent some fundamental changes. Out of the defeat arose a new kind of collective mysticism, more patriotic in tone. A "national messianism" began to take shape.[8]

Between the end of the XIXth and the early XXth century, a new form of collective mysticism with messianic overtones emerged among the clerical elite. Mgr. Laflèche, and later to a lesser extent, Canon Lionel Groulx, prophesied a messianic role for the French Catholic people of North America. They proclaimed that the French-Canadians were destined to be the chosen people of God. They exhorted the population to obedience to the Church in return for a glorious call to the promised land. Mgr. Laflèche compared the plight of the French-Canadian people to Israel. For him "American France . . . is nothing other than the New Israel of God since it is the heir of the Old France and therefore the heir to the promises made to the Church, and the promise made before that to Israel."[9]

As we have seen already, colonialism has broad and sometimes ill effects on the culture it is imposed upon. Extensive ethnological studies show that when cultures are oppressed by a foreign power they instigate movements of messianic salvation, some with revolutionary goals.[10] In some cases, the revolt takes the guise of a religious movement but ends in violent outbursts. The conquest and later the defeat of the Rebellion of 1837-38 inhibited the "normal" evolution of the national identity. The strong sense of religious conviction inspired by the Church led the people to shift their desire for national freedom into a mystic vision upheld as a "national messianism".

---

[8] Gabriel Dussault, L'Eglise A-t-Elle "Oublié" ses Promesses?, in, *Relations,* 386, 1973, 264-267.

[9] G. Dussault, Ibid. 266.

[10] See reference on messianism and bibliography, p. 93.

As a result, the ideological boundaries that usually exist between what is believed to be strictly nationalistic and religious fade. National aspirations become intertwined with deep expressions of collective mysticism. The messianic movement described above reinforces the "distinct" calling of its people and polarizes even further the gap between the French and the English mold of cultural differences and divisions.

collective asceticism	vs	secular asceticism
French language	vs	English language
Catholics	vs	Protestants
farmers	vs	merchants
labor	vs	industrialist

At this point, it is crucial to stress the importance of the dynamic of **opposition** in the development of a national identity. The antagonism separates and reinforces the cultural differences. As we have explained already, the stronger the opposition, the greater the belief in the sacred identity.

•

Although the Catholic Church imposed on its believers a stoic acceptance of the political reality of the British rule, it nevertheless fought any form of assimilation. While the Church was preaching a passive submission to the English rule, it maintained a strong sense of cultural identity. Since the Conquest of 1760, the Church had promoted among its faithful the urgency of its collective survival. Under its guidance the people were kept together by two things: *la langue et la foi;* eg, the French language and faith. Both were instruments of social unity and a barrier against foreign intrusion. They became the two main vehicles for social integration. They are still the two major components of contemporary nationalism.

•

Language and a desire for emancipation have been vital forces behind the renewal of nationalism that began in the nineteen sixties. As the nationalist movement began to spread, the Quebec society underwent rapid cultural changes. The Quebec people perceived themselves as "other" and "apart" from the rest of Canada. It is this perceived sense of distinctness that allowed the "separatists" to make political headway among *le peuple québécois.*

As the "Spirit" of renewal and openness swept Vatican II, Quebec society as a whole was undergoing its own "Quiet Revolution". In less than a decade, the power of the Church eroded. Meanwhile, political changes were spreading throughout society. The educational system, formally the stronghold of the Church, was rapidly becoming secularized. The medical system, under the control of the clerical hierarchy, was nationalized. Little by little, Quebec society became more secular. Secularization was undertaken so swiftly that it appeared as if the people wanted to be rid of the heavy moral burden the Church had imposed on them during the last two centuries.

Simultaneously, from the late fifties and throughout the sixties, television took center stage in a majority of homes. People indiscriminately plugged into the power of its message. TV began to shatter the mold of the insular mind as it opened a window to the outside world. Inadvertently, this medium began to challenge the old religious and cultural models by the power of its images. Its mass appeal precipitated even further the secularization of society. The images presented on TV eventually supplanted the ethical models preached by the Church. The Chapel was no longer the center for the "Word".

Until the sixties, business signs in Montreal were predominantly in English, reflecting the Anglo-Saxon economic control over the city. It revealed the disproportionate supremacy of the minority over the French majority. Things would rapidly change.

As the desire for emancipation grew, a new wave of radical nationalism arose. The new breed of nationalists demanded more control of their political and economical destinies. They felt, with reason, that their language and culture were threatened by the overwhelming Anglo-Saxon presence in North-America.

An alarming decrease in the French birthrate and a dramatic increase in the immigration of people who would rather learn English sparked fears of assimilation. Quebec, the only bastion of French language and culture in America, was threatened. In the late sixties and early seventies, radical movements like the F.L.Q.—*Front de Libération du Québec*—undertook to promote social awareness about such threats. The radical movement advocated complete political control over the province's destiny. Among their demands was the **separation** of Quebec from the rest of Canada. To show that they were serious, they planted bombs in the mail boxes—a symbol of the Federal Government—of the affluent English section of Montreal.

From the more radical *Rassemblement pour l'indépendance nationale* (R.I.N.), emerged a moderate *indépendantiste* party under the leadership of René Lévesque, a former Liberal provincial cabinet member.[11] The movement appealed to the masses as it revived memories of broken dreams and shattered hopes. The promise of

---

[11] Under the leadership of Liberal Prime Minister Jean Lesage.

independence rang out as a clear message of liberation. To implement these goals, the *Parti Québécois* (P.Q.) proposed the option of "sovereignty-association" with the "rest" of Canada.

Quebec	vs	Canada
Parti Québécois	vs	Liberal Party of Canada
French	vs	English

The idea of independence rekindled memories of lost aspirations. It captured the hearts of the people who longed to transcend their past. It allowed them to hail their own future. As such, the movement inspired what the more radical nationalist detractors derisively called "the religion of René".[12]

To promote the idea of independence, the P.Q. used metaphors like "paradise" and warned against "old demons" and "abortionists" that opposed their goal.[13] People who were close to René Lévesque were called the "evangelists". One of his closest ministers was even described as "the disciple that René Lévesque loved". These quasi-messianic references consecrated even further the cause in which they believed. The leader himself became the embodiment of a sacred mission of "quasi-religious" proportion.[14] The collective passion among its members became vivid and intense as the nationalists became spirited by its crusade. The **quest** for independence became more and more **mythical** in meaning and function as the movement grew more popular among a greater segment of the population.

•

The historical development of nationalism outlines the desire to be "distinct". It prompted opposition to whoever challenged this assumption. The dynamic opposition to the **other** cultural entity reinforced the Quebecers' sense of **conviction** in their own "separate" identity. What existed outside the periphery of the linguistic and religious boundaries—*la langue et la foi*—was considered a threat to the social makeup. As we have already explained in previous chapters, the stronger the antagonism to the outer cultural reality, the greater the inner identity. This opposition first began with the **profane** reality of the heathen, which was an obstacle

---

[12] See Peter Desbarats', René, Toronto, Seal Books, 1977, 192.

[13] Political Pamphlet, *Quand Nous Serons Vraiment Chez-Nous*.

[14] Paul Tillich, Christianity and the Encounter of the World Religions, New York, Columbia University Press, 1963.

179

to colonization, and eventually, it was transposed into the **struggle** against the English **adversary.**[15]

The French language became the main bond among the people. It also became a communication barrier against *les anglais.* Religion, on the other hand, further consolidated the conviction of "distinct" identity as Catholics. The mythical quest for **independence** became the noetic integrator of the Quebecers. These thematic symbols captured the core of the "historical" experience of the people. It originated from a legitimate desire to recreate a golden age, a "Paradise Lost", if you will, that was denied to them by history. Independence became the rallying icon of that legitimate desire.

It is one of history's paradox that as soon as the secularization took hold in Quebec, nationalistic concerns arose. What was unique about the people of Quebec prior to the nineteen sixties was the strength of their separate religious identity as well as their language. The province was the only bastion of French Catholicism in North America. The ensuing spiritual vacuum that came as a result of people leaving the Church propelled the faithful quest to be "distinct" in a secularized world. As a consequence, the collective mentality was politicized. Yet the advent of the political and cultural emancipation of French society also increased the danger of assimilation into the greater North American melting pot. As a remedy, a dose of nationalism was embodied by the quest for independence.

As we have tried to show above, the mythical aspect of history thrives in the minds of the people who are deeply affected by its significance. The quest for independence embodies the collective spirit of the people in search of their own integrity and identity.

There is yet another paradox. The very essence of the *québécois'* **identity** was instigated by the **antagonism** toward the **"other"** cultural entities: first, versus the natives, and then, the English. In other words, the essence of Quebec's distinctiveness stems from the **opposition** to English Canada. Without it, the core of its identity might be unpredictably altered.

---

[15] Ironically, today Quebec with only a quarter of the country's population turns out 40% of the business school graduates of Canada. In 1988, the province yielded half of the 50 fastest growing, publicly-held companies in the nation. It is a characteristic of antagonist acculturation for cultures to finally embrace wholeheartedly the cultural principles that they opposed at the outset. See George Devereux on "antagonist acculturation" in, Ethnopsychanalyse Complémentariste, Paris, Flamarion, 1972, 201-231.

THE WASHINGTON NATIONAL MONUMENT: The Myth Making of America

In an earlier study on the dedication of Quebec's monuments, I realized that these civil events revealed interesting details about the mythical edification of society as a whole.[1] Consequently, I chose to expand my field of research to include at least one of the major U.S. monuments. My goal in doing this is to reveal how the process of dedication of the Washington National Monument, in Washington D.C., is kindred to American civil religion and how it is a mythological showcase of the U.S.' ideological foundation. As we shall see, the dedication of monuments is a privileged ritual that discloses the consecration of American civil religion in society.[2] By the same token, these ceremonials reveal how America's most celebrated political hero yields a mythological significance of primal importance.[3] It also reveals how the exclusion of the Goddess principle from Judeo-Christianism through the centuries promoted the creation of a hierarchical and patriarchal New World order.

---

[1] I turned my attention to this subject in my Masters' thesis entitled: Interprétation Religeuse de l'Origine Mythique de la Nationalité: L'Inauguration de Monuments Nationaux (1840-1900), Montréal, UQAM, 1978.

[2] Robert N. Bellah, The Broken Covenant: American Civil Religion in Time of Trial, New York, Seabury Press, 1975; and Beyond Belief; Essays on Religion in a Post-Traditional World, New York, Harper & Row, 1970.

[3] The whole ceremony is related in Frederick Harvey's, ed., History of the Washington National Monument & Washington National Monument Society, Washington D.C., Government Printing Office, 1903.

185

We will take a close look at two aspects of the inauguration: the ritual and the mythical. The first deals with the festivities of the ceremony that act as an introduction to the orators and their speeches. The second relates to the content of the speeches themselves which eulogize, better yet, mythologize the hero to whom the monument is dedicated.

At the inauguration, the hero whose identity is immortalized in the stone is literally consecrated by the monument. The people who congregate for the ceremony recreate a time of vital significance in history. By the same token, the audience—the elected representatives of society as a whole—endorses the hero as a national figure who is chosen as a prototype of American political foundation. By their presence they acknowledge the hero's meaningful legacy to history.

As we have seen earlier, the discovery and foundation of a new territory has a mythological significance. The **first** to discover a new land, or the **first** president of a new political reality is a primal event of historical and mythological significance. His name and his role in American history has a unique place **above** all other historical figures and events.

Thus, the Washington National Monument was erected to celebrate the primordial in the United States' history, similar in fashion to the erection of temples and sacred buildings dedicated for the most sacred purposes. In that respect, the Monument becomes **central** in American history. To use Mircea Eliade's words, the Monument becomes an *axis mundi*.[4] The "axis" from which everything began and from where everything flows. As such, the Washington National Monument symbolizes the beginning of the nation's political history built at the **center** of the political power of the United States of America.

The type of monument chosen is fitting. Nothing could have better represented the hero's grandeur. No monument could have been more adequate to express how central the **hero** is to American history and politics. Moreover, the shaft could not have been more appropriate to symbolize the idea of the **center** and **patriarchy.**

The type of structure and the site were specifically chosen to reflect a symbolic and mythical expression. The people responsible for this task were concerned about finding the most appropriate place.

---

[4] Mircea Eliade, Cosmos and History, New York, Harper & Row, 1959, 12.

It may be here remarked, with reference to the site selected for the Monument, that the foundations were laid but a short distance to the east of the meridian line run, at the instance of the President Jefferson, by Nicholas King, surveyor, October 15, 1804 . . . This line, by the president's instructions, passed through the **center** of the White House, and where it intersected a line due east and west through the **center** of the Capitol a small monument or pyramid of stones was placed . . .[5]

The center yields an important symbolic significance in most mythologies. As a sacred space it stands **apart** from the ordinariness of its surrounding. In the world of mythology, the *axis mundi* is represented in different forms: a tree, a mountain, a ladder, or a pillar. Yet they all symbolize the **communication** between the two cosmic arenas: heaven and earth, and the center and its periphery.

Similarly, the Holy of Holies was at the center of the temple of Jerusalem, also considered to be at the center of the world. In Greek mythology, the shrine of Apollo at Delphi was also declared the earth's center. For Islam, Jerusalem is equally the center of its faith, and the Muslim Dome of the Rock is the sacred place from where the prophet Muhammed ascended to heaven.[6]

•

In its proportions the ratios of the dimensions of the several parts of the ancient Egyptian obelisk have been carefully followed.[7]

These remarks by Col. Thomas Lincoln Casey, chief engineer in charge of the Monument, were made to reveal that it was to be a larger replica of an Egyptian obelisk—an erected stone carved into a four sided pillar crowned with a small pyramid called the pyramidion. The Washington National Monument is a much larger replica than the original obelisks found in Egypt. These were made out of a single block of rock, whereas the capital's structure is made of 36,000 blocks of stone.

The Egyptians usually erected the obelisks in pairs in front of Egyptian temples. They were believed to be sacred. Scholars are still uncertain about their specific use or function. Obelisks are neverthe-

---

[5] Ibid. F. Harvey, 43. Taken from the National Geographic Magazine, vol. 6, 149.

[6] In myths, the hill and the moutain are important places where the earth and the heavens meet. It is where the divine greet the human, where the above touch the below, and the sacred and the profane converge.

[7] Ibid. F. Harvey, 224.

less a unique symbol of Egyptian culture. Romans wcrc so fascinated by the pillars that they moved several of them to Rome where some still stand today.

In ancient Egypt, the pyramidion that crowned the monolith was probably covered with gold to reflect the sun's rays.[8] The pyramidion, in all likelihood, also crowned the great pyramids of Egypt. Technically, the obelisk symbolizes a ray of light emanating from the sun. The pointed pillars were perhaps relevant symbols of light and life, and the daily course of the sun as opposed to the pyramids that were symbols of darkness and death, and the setting sun. The earliest obelisks are believed to have been erected in the 4th dynasty (*circa* 2613-2494 BC). No examples from that era remain today.

In the late 19th century, the government of Egypt gave one of the two Ramses' obelisks ornating the Luxor temple to France where it stands in Paris' Place de la Concorde. Two other obelisks were shipped to England and to the United States. Both were taken from Heliopolis. They were dedicated to Thutmose III and bear the inscriptions and legends of two pharaohs: Thutmose III, and Ramses II (1304-1237 BC). One stands on the Thames' embankment, in London, the other is in Central Park, in New York City.

The connection between the Washington National Monument and the gift from Egypt is, to say the least, a suitable symbol of the continuity between an ancient civilization and an emerging one.

History of the Monument

The Washington National Monument Society was founded in 1833 because Congress did not keep its promise to erect a monument deserving of the national hero. Several unsuccessful attempts were made to collect the necessary funds before the Society took over. And it was not until 1884 that the Monument was finally completed.

In 1853, Congress appropriated $50,000 for the erection of an "equestrian statue" of George Washington. It was unveiled on February 22nd 1860 in the east park of the Capitol. The Society viewed the statue as unworthy of the national hero and persevered to build a monument equal in stature to George Washington.

In 1835, two years after the foundation of the Society, its first president, John Marshall, died and was replaced by the ex-president

---

[8] For more about the obelisks of Egypt see Labib Habachi's, The Obelisks of Egypt, Cairo, American University in Cairo Press, 1984.

of the United States, James Madison. Upon the death of James Madison, the Society amended its constitution so that the president in office became *ex-officio* president of the Society. Andrew Jackson was the first to honor this function under the newly amended constitution.

On the 4th of July 1848, the first cornerstone was laid. To celebrate the occasion a ceremony was organized.

By January 1853, the Monument had risen 126 feet above ground.

On March 8th, 1854, a block of marble sent by Pope Pius IX as a tribute to George Washington and America that was to be part of the giant structure, was stolen.[9] The suspicion quickly pointed toward a group known as the "Know-Nothings". A secretive anti-Catholic political movement, who at the time enjoyed considerable Masonic support.[10] The group had frequently expressed in the daily press the view that the stone sent by the Roman Catholic Church should not be part of the Monument. The theft enraged the Catholics in the U.S. and abroad. It also alienated part of the population from the funding of the Monument.

The Society subsequently fell at the hands of a narrow political faction influenced by the "Know-Nothings". It practically froze the progress of the Society toward the funding and construction of the Monument. Finally, in February of 1859 the Society decided to end its internal stalemate and adopted a new charter to eliminate any opposition to the completion of their project.

One year later, the Civil War further delayed progress in the construction.

The war and the poor state of the economy slowed the collection of funds and the completion of the Monument. Not until 1874 did the construction gain any momentum. It was largely due to the interest of the Masonic Order and other organizations like the Odd Fellows, the Knights of Pythias, the Independent Order of Red Men, the Temperance, and other fraternal bodies. But the success of the enterprise was mostly owed to the special interest of the Masonic Order who supervised the completion of the Monument.

On December 6th, 1884, the giant structure was finally completed. The last piece of stone was put atop the marble shaft measuring 555 feet and 5 inches.

---

[9] The same year the Immaculate Conception became an article of faith.

[10] The movement also fought unsuccessfully to minimize the anti-slavery sentiments of that time.

On February 21st, 1885, the Capitol proceeded to the dedication of the Washington National Monument. All of the capital's dignitaries were present as Rev. Henderson Suter said a prayer at the beginning of the ceremonies. Shortly after, a Masonic function took place at the base of the Monument, followed by the address of the Grand Master Mason, Myron M. Parker. The dedication was completed by the oration of Hon. Robert C. Winthrop.

It shouldn't come as a surprise to see the Grand Master Mason at the laying of the cornerstone and later at the inauguration of the Monument. The organization played a sizable part in the collection of the funds to build the structure. But there is another reason for the brotherhood's interest in the building and their overwhelming presence at the ceremonies. George Washington was himself a Freemason.

The dedication

The great show that is the dedication enables us to unveil how the mythical and the ritual work hand in hand in the building of the national identity. The greater the hero, the larger the ceremony, and the bigger the monument. The rank and stature of dignitaries is also akin to the grandeur of the hero. Everything is planned carefully. The order of the march, the sequence of the orators, the speeches, the music, and the dramatic display of the festivities. But the most important feature of the dedication are the **speeches** themselves. The orators have put forth their best **rhetoric** abilities to eulogize the hero in all his glory.

Appropriately enough, the first president of the United States of America and the origins of rhetoric have something in common: democracy.

The first rules of rhetoric appear to have begun in Syracuse, circa 500 BC. When exiles returned to their homeland after being dispossessed of their property by a despotic ruler, they had no written records to prove the ownership of their property to the new government. In order to solve the disputes, a newly democratic system of debate was devised where verbal claims of ownership could be settled. To help the litigants improve their **persuasiveness,** teachers, some of them Sophists, developed rules of elocution and persuasiveness. As a result, a new discipline was born: rhetoric. The term comes from the Greek word *rhēma* which was later translated into Latin as *verbum,* meaning **word.**[11]

---

[11] Rhetoric was later developed by Aristotle in works like RHETORIC and TOPICS. It

The discipline eventually evolved into the "science" of speaking effectively so to persuade an audience. At about the same time that the Monument was being built, rhetoric was being dropped from the *cursus studiorum* in the colleges of Europe. In the second half of the XIXth century, classical rhetoric lost its appeal in the schools as a general discipline. Lately, however, there has been a resurgence of interest in the subject.[12]

•

Although the Monument is a visible relic that everyone can see, the dramatic effect of the ceremony cannot be reproduced. The only thing that remains for us is an account of the festivities and the record of the speeches. Frederich Harvey's account in "History of the Washington National Monument and Washington Monument Society", published in 1903, holds tremendous value for our study. And although the speeches are devoid of the rhetorical effect of the delivery, their content is a valuable data for analysis. The book reveals the important aspects of the ritualization and mythologizing process of the **image** of the First President and the Founding Father of the United States of America.

The primal function of rhetoric is to make a speech as convincing as possible, making the content plausible and believable. Yet the ultimate purpose is to convince the audience to believe in the sacred validity of the Founding Father. To achieve these goals the Romans had three principles of elocution: *docere, delectare,* and *movere:* namely, to teach, to captivate, and to move the audience.

These functions are also applied to the sermon, from the Latin *sermo* meaning to talk. Similarly, Rabbis use their rhetorical abilities to "instruct" the law. The Koran is most efficient and most beautiful when it is read aloud. In Zen Buddhism, the verbal use of paradox, or *koans,* is most enchanting when spoken. And the elocution of the *Tao te Ching* of Taoism is considered to be the most beautiful form of expression of the Chinese language. Furthermore, Jesus Christ did not write his message, he proclaimed it. The kerygma of the **Word** is most effective when it is preached. It is quintessential

---

eventually became the means of putting into practice, especially with the help of argumentation, the wisdom one acquires in philosophy. Later, the art was most skillfully applied by the Roman master orator and statesman Cicero, as described in his *De Oratore* (55 BC). In the first century AD, rhetoric became the subject of an important educational treatise entitled *Instituto oratoria* by the Roman Quintinllian. It evolved until the middle of the XIXth century into a major educational discipline and one of the seven liberal arts. But, as the last century faded, rhetoric as a "general" science was slowly being supplanted by the increasingly popular natural sciences. See Walter J. Ong, Orality and Literacy, New York, Methuen, 1982; and, Rhetoric, Romance, and Technology, Ithaca, Cornell University Press, 1971.

[12] See Paul Ricoeur, The Rule of Metaphor, Toronto, University of Toronto Press, 1977.

in the **propagation** of faith. Similarly, political speeches are essential in the **propaganda** of ideology.

Hence, the "word" is used to promote and edify a reality in the mind of the people who listen.

Today, the mass-media applies similar techniques in advertising to influence their audience.

The speeches

Harvey's document accounts for two ceremonies. The first, at the beginning, at the laying of the first cornerstone, and the second, at the completion of the superstructure. Both are equal in importance, yet are 37 years apart.

The first ceremony was celebrated on the 4th of July 1848. For the occasion, the president of the United States, James K. Polk, and dignitaries of the capital were present, as well as Senators, Representatives of Congress, the Military, delegations from the States, and several "Indian" tribes. In addition, 15,000 to 20,000 spectators were all gathered for the festivities. On that day, the initial stone, a block of marble weighing twenty-four thousand five hundred pounds, was laid.

The following is a newspaper excerpt that describes the mood of the festivities:

> The day was fine. The rain had laid the dust and infused a delicious freshness in the air. The procession was extensive and beautiful . . . When the lengthened procession had reached the site of the Monument they were joined by a whole cortège of ladies and gentlemen; and we are free to say we never beheld so magnificent a spectacle.[13]

The whole setting has a central goal: to focus the attention on the speeches that recreate the life and image of the hero who is the object of the celebration. These eulogies, also called panegyric, have for their sole purpose to glorify and consecrate the Founding Father. The rhetorical function is to influence the audience to collectively hail the national hero.

The whole gathering is besieged by the sacredness of the event. As the speeches affect the crowd, the crowd in return collectively sanctions the message. In the process, the image of George Washington is mythically anointed as a primordial hero, vital to the nation's

---

[13] Ibid. F. Harvey, 46.

identity. As the Monument that stands erected toward the heavens in the background, the orators proclaim the hero a primordial symbol, visible to all.

The man *is* the monument; the monument *is* America.[14]

The ceremony began with a prayer delivered by Rev. Mr. McJilton. In it he outlined the purpose of the dedication: "We plant in earth the shaft that points to heaven". A tribute to the man who was the instrument of God in the fight for freedom. The Reverend also disclosed his concern for peace. He expressed his apprehension about the "union". And he condemned the "savages of the wilderness" as an obstacle to the free exploitation of the "unknown treasures" and "limitless territory to the industry and enterprise of man".

The Reverend also mentioned "Thy church" without reference to any specific creed, except that it is "of a certain faith". He concluded by asking the blessings and mediation of Jesus Christ, "our most blessed Lord and Saviour. Amen."

The prayer was followed by an oration from Honorable Robert C. Winthrop, Speaker of the House of Representatives. It is the main speech of the ceremonial. Winthrop was presumably a man of renowned oratorical skills since he was to be invited to the dedication 37 years later.

the setting	America
the hero	Washington, Father of his Country
the quest	Liberty and Independence
the obstacle	treacherous enemies
the mentor	Divine Providence
the outcome	the Republic and its Constitution

His speech is similar in content and in tone to the Reverend's eulogy. He repeated and expanded on the same themes, most of which are summarized in the thematic outline above.

The first category relates to the origin of the American nation and its politics, of which George Washington is the chief protagonist. The New World is the stage for the hero's actions which were guided by Divine Providence: they led to the Revolution and the Constitution of the United States of America. In his quality of first president, he is hailed as the original founder, the **Father** of his Country.

---

[14] Marcus Cunliffe, George Washington, Man and Monument, Boston, Little, Brown Co., 1958, 213.

The elocution refers to the General by different designations, several of which have already been mentioned. Other titles point to the more ethereal quality of the man: The "idol", the "favorite of heaven" who yielded a "magic power" and "majestic authority".

His star has been seen in every sky, and wise men everywhere have done it homage.[15]

The hero's quest outlines a desire for Liberty and Independence. Washington is the embodiment of these goals in the midst of the colonial struggle.

The obstacles to his pursuit are refered to as the foreign powers, the wilderness, the heathen "Indians", and the treacherous enemies that he victoriously overcomes by his personal prowess.

The mentor is depicted as the Providence, the Great Spirit, and the Divine Hand that guides the illustrious hero at all times.

The outcome is stated as:

He has built his own monument. We, and those who come after us in successive generations, are its appointed, its privileged guardians. This widespread Republic is the true monument to Washington. Maintain its Independence. Uphold its Constitution. Preserve its Union. Defend its liberty.[16]

As soon as the Honorable Robert C. Winthrop finished his eulogy, he was followed on the podium by Mr. Benjamin B. French Esq., Grand Master of the Masonic fraternity of the District of Columbia, who began by saying:

Why have we assembled here to-day (sic)? What means this immense crowd around us? For what,, beneath a July sun, on this anniversary of the birthday of a nation, has this vast multitude come up, as came Israel of old to the dedication of the Temple of the Lord?[17]

The rest of the speech reiterates the same themes that we have outlined above, with the exception of stressing the fact that the first president was a Freemason.

---

[15] Ibid. F. Harvey, 126.

[16] Ibid. F. Harvey, 130.

[17] Ibid. F. Harvey, 136.

After his speech, he descended to the cornerstone and performed a Masonic ceremony at the laying of it.

•

The dedication, unlike the festivities at the laying of the first cornerstone, were performed at two locations. It all began at the foot of the Monument and continued in a long procession toward the Capitol into the Hall of the House of Representatives.

The first part of the festivities began at 11 o'clock on February the 21st, 1885. The celebrations took place in the presence of a great number of visitors from all parts of the country. The chairman of the Commission, Hon. John Sherman, presided over the order of the proceedings while the band played on. The first to step on the podium was Rev. Henderson Suter who said a prayer. He was followed by Dr. James who read a speech written by W.W. Corcoran.[18] Then, Myron Parker, the Grand Master of the Grand Lodge of the District of Columbia, performed his Masonic ceremonies and delivered his address. He was followed by the engineer of the joint commission, Col. Thomas L. Casey, who made some remarks about the construction of the giant structure before he delivered the Monument to the president of the United States. Finally, President Chester A. Arthur gave a very brief speech dedicating the Monument to the "immortal name and memory of George Washington".[19]

Surprisingly, the dedication was not as elaborate as the laying of the cornerstone. The most interesting part is the peculiar Masonic ceremony performed by Myron M. Parker: the Most Worshipful Grand Master of the Grand Lodge of Free and Accepted Masons of the District of Columbia. The brief example below illustrates the dialogue used by the members of the order for their ritual:

GRAND MASTER. Right Worshipful Deputy Grand Master, what is the proper implement of your office?

DEPUTY GRAND MASTER. The square, Most Worshipful.

GRAND MASTER. What are its moral and Masonic uses?

DEPUTY GRAND MASTER. To square our actions by square virtue, and prove our work when finished.

GRAND MASTER. Have you applied the square to the obelisk, and is the work square?

---

[18] The speech is not included in Harvey's book.

[19] Ibid. F. Harvey, 104-105. For some unknown reason the president's dedication was overshadowed by the other addresses.

DEPUTY GRAND MASTER. I have, and I find the corners to be square; the workmen have done their duty . . . [20]

After the ritual, the Grand Master gave his address. In it, he described how George Washington was a most distinguished brethren who had openly expressed his love and devotion for the Order throughout his life.

•

As the first part of the festivities ended, the crowd followed the dignitaries in a procession to the Capitol, clearly visible at a distance. They were escorted by the Army and the Navy. The parade is described as being imposing.

At the Capitol, all the dignitaries were gathered in the Hall of the House of Representatives for the official dedication. The president of the Senate, Hon. George F. Edmunds, presided. He called the assembly to order. He introduced the Rev. S.A. Wallis who offered a prayer.

Then, Hon. John D. Long, a representative from Massachusetts, was introduced. He read an oration written by the same Hon. Robert C. Winthrop who had delivered a speech at the opening ceremonies, thirty seven years earlier. He was unable to attend due to illness.

In between the orations, lively music was performed by the United States Marine Band.

The content of Winthrop's address is basically the same as the earlier one. The veneration given to the ''immortal name of Washington'' can be singly noted:

The glory of Columbus can never be eclipsed, never approached, till our **New World** shall require a fresh discovery; and the glory of Washington will remain unique and peerless until American Independence shall require to be again achieved, or the foundations of Constitutional Liberty to be laid anew. [22]

It was followed by a speech from Hon. John W. Daniel, of Virginia, who rendered an ''eloquent'' oration. He described with verve the great qualities of the national hero:

---

[20] Ibid. F. Harvey, 214.
[22] Ibid. F. Harvey, 252.

. . . the genius of Washington was as full-orbed and luminous as the god of day in his zenith.[23]

He explained to the assembly that the glorious hero was full of his ancestors' qualities of a "higher and manlier trait of the Anglo-Saxon".

The proceedings came to a close. At the end of which a short benediction was pronounced by Rev. John A. Lindsay D.D., chaplain of the House of Representatives.

The blessing of God Almighty, the Father, the Son, and the Holy Spirit, be among you and remain with you always. Amen.[24]

The image of George Washington

The mere mention of the name George Washington can easily stir lively feelings of pride and patriotism in the hearts of Americans. These emotions are hard to explain and describe. Yet the devotion is tangible. Men have died and killed for these feelings. They are at the core of what it means to be **American.**

The hero's image unleashes patriotic sentiments that are a powerful source of pride and national identity. With George Washington, the image is immortalized in the monumental stone. The mortal man has become **other** than man. The ordinary being is transcended into an immortal hero erected at the political center of the U.S. He is literally consecrated as the **symbol** of America's political identity. His symbolic image has eclipsed the mundane reality of his being. The mortal has been **separated** from the immortal which is embodied in the Monument.

The symbolic reality of the Founding Father has overlapped the historical into the mythical. With the dedication he has been consecrated as "more than man". The heroic and mythical aspects of the figure have transcended and supplanted the historical. As a consequence, Washington's name suggests not only images of the hero but a reality bigger than life, an unfathomable entity: the center of political power of the United States of America and the content of an entire cosmology. And the Monument is its **metaphor.**

•

Soon after Washington's death, in 1799, at about the same time that the Monument was being commissioned, a great deal of atten-

[23] Ibid. F. Harvey, 278.

[24] Ibid. F. Harvey, 285.

tion by the country's Anglo-Saxon elite was focussed on the image of the first president. His death swiftly buried criticism concerning any misgivings about his life as a general, and as a president. He soon became the subject of a nationwide movement of eulogies meant to aggrandize his personal standing. As the nation made its first steps toward finding its national identity, George Washington became more and more the focus of a country-wide image making campaign.

Numerous books were written about his exemplary life. THE LIFE OF WASHINGTON, written by Mason Locke Weems of Dumfries, Virginia, is a typical example of the "myth-maker" of that era.[25] The movement lasted throughout the century and Weems' book became the prototype for many other biographies that "deified" the "Father hero". Soon, George Washington was not only described as a father figure, but as "more than man", and as an "immortal Olympian". His image transcended that of national hero to become in many ways that of a mythical "Father". Authors and orators were not content to merely extol his image above all other heroes, some even compared Washington to Christ and his mother to the Virgin Mary.[26]

Among the vast number of biographies of the era, especially those written before 1855, one could easily be led to believe that Washington was a demigod who descended on earth with the sole purpose of creating a new country and freeing its people, and then returned to heaven as soon as his mission was accomplished.[27]

The views outlined above show how the mythical and historical processes work hand in hand in the edification of a national identity, and how the boundaries between the two are blurred. These processes were further endorsed by a collective appropriation and recognition of the American hero. The cultural identification set the standards for a social consensus that became central to the development of the country's identity. As such, the mythologizing of George Washington played a central role in the integration of the American political reality.

---

[25] Mason Locke Weems, The Life of Washington, ed. Marcus Cunliffe, Cambridge, Harvard University Press, 1962.

[26] Bernard Mayo, Myths and Men, Athens, University of Georgia Press, 1959, 33, and the whole chapter on Washington, 25-49.

[27] William A. Bryan, George Washington in American Literature, 1775-1865, New York, Columbia University Press, 1952, 118. Also, Richard V. Pierard & Robert D. Linder, Civil Religion & the Presidency, Grand Rapids, Academie Books, 1988.

Washington the Freemason

The ceremonies we have described are revealing in many ways. At both festivities a representative of the Freemasonry was present to honor their illustrious brethren. Not unusual, since the brotherhood played a substantial part in the funding of the structure. But the Monument is also a great architectural salute to the **Masons** themselves. It is a worthy tribute to the first president of the United States who was also a brethren.

George Washington was the first, but not the last, president to be a Freemason. Several past presidents of the United States have been Freemasons, from George Washington to Ronald Reagan, as well as 9 signers of the Declaration of Independence and 13 signers of the Constitution.[28]

In addition, many other heroes of the American Revolution were also Masons; Paul Revere and John Hancock are only two examples. Benjamin Franklin was also a leader of the Freemasonry in Pennsylvania, and published the first Masonic book in America in 1734.

•

To fully understand the foundations of America's mythical process, a few words about the origin of the elusive Brotherhood are in order.

It evolved from the stonemason guilds of England and Scotland. When the major building projects—mostly churches and cathedrals of Europe—came to an end, several stonemasons who did not practice their skills any longer stayed on in the fraternal association and formed lodges, the name given to their basic unit. The first lodges were founded in London, England, in the late XVIIIth century. It is at that epoch that "architecture" acquired a more metaphorical sense. The grandiose stone buildings began to symbolize human structures, reflecting an ideal humanity built "to the glory of the Great Architect of the Universe".

More legendary stories attribute the origin of Masonry to the Garden of Eden. While other versions link its beginning to the building of the **pyramids** of Egypt, and to Hiram Abif, King Solomon's Master Architect, the legendary builder of the first temple of Jerusalem.

---

[28] They are: George Washington, James Madison, James Monroe, Andrew Jackson, James Knox Polk, James Buchanan, Andrew Johnson, James A. Garfield, William McKinley, both Roosevelts, William H. Taft, Warren G. Harding, Harry S. Truman, Lyndon Johnson, Gerald Ford, Richard Nixon and Ronald Reagan.

Currently, there are more than 6 million Freemasons in the world.[29] Most of them live in the U.S. and Canada. As a nonsectarian and nonpolitical association, the fraternity appeals to a wide cross section of the male population. They believe in a Supreme Being and emphasize the **fatherhood** of God and the brotherhood of man. Freemasons are said to admit in their rank men of every nationality, religion, and political persuasion. In order to join, a new member must be introduced by an existing brethren.

Most of the operations and activities of the Society are shrouded by an aura of mystery. Most of it results from the oath of secrecy they must make in regards to the identity of its members.

The early American brotherhood was able to survive an anti-Masonic wave following the abduction and possible murder of Captain William Morgan in 1826. Morgan had planned to publish an article about Masonic secret dealings. Evidence of his murder was linked to the Masons. The public outcry against the organization lasted 10 years and slowly boiled down afterward.

During World War II, the Masons were outlawed and dispersed by Stalin, Mussolini, Hitler, and Franco. After the war, they soon regained their popularity in non-communist countries, particularly, the United States.

Among its most popular members: Wolfgang Amadeus Mozart, Henry Ford, Charles A. Lindbergh, Irving Berlin, Gen. Douglas McArthur, John Wayne, J. Edgar Hoover, Richard Nixon, and Ronald Reagan.

Because of its Anglo-Saxon origins, nineteenth century Masonry in the U.S. might convey the idea that the order was predominantly male, white, Anglo-Saxon and Protestant. But a closer look at a cross-section of its members reveals that a more accurate description would be: a white, generally non-Catholic, male organization. In San Francisco of last century, for instance, most of the Jewish adult male population belonged to the brotherhood. Which prompted an anonymous Jewish brethren to write, in 1865, in the San Francisco's *Hebrew:*

If there be any religious system more closely connected with the institution [of Masonry] than others, *it is Judaism.*[30]

---

[29] In 1964 the Masonic Order enrolled about 1 out of every 12 men in the U.S.

[30] "Perhaps the most surprising representatives in the Masonic non-evangelical alliance were the large number of Jews. In Gilded-Age San Francisco, Jews comprised 12% of the brotherhood's membership, about the same proportion which they formed in the city's adult, white, male, non-Catholic population as a whole. Considering the strictly Protestant origins of Freemasonry, this high proportion of Jewish members is extraordinary." Carl

Although the order claims to be open to all races and all religions, the American lodges refused to initiate any "Negro" as a brethren and rejected the legitimacy of any "Negro" Masonic lodges. In 1775, the Grand Lodge of England instigated the first lodge of "Negroes" in Boston, which eventually assumed the status of grand lodge and chartered other "Negro" Prince Hall lodges. Today, relations between the white and the American of African descent lodges have improved.

During the time the Monument was built, the organization was mostly a middle class order that mirrored the mores and mentality of the epoch: piety, sobriety, moral responsibility, thrift, and industry. In many respects, it exemplified the Protestant ethic at its best.

The *raison d'être* of the brotherhood was to promote charity, equality, fraternity, morality, and faith in the Supreme Being. It supplied its members with a sense of fraternity, prestige, and occasionally financial aid. It also provided business connections and networking. On a national level, Masons claimed among its members presidents, senators, and other dignitaries, who established the rules for accessibility in the political arena.

The fraternity's activities however were not entirely reclusive and esoteric. The order also participated in social events. A typical example here is the role they played in the ceremonies at the inauguration of the Washington Monument. Another example of their social acceptance and popularity is further evidenced by their participation at the laying of the cornerstone of the Statue of Liberty, in 1885.

Sociologically, the Masonry reflected the craze for associations, brotherhoods, fraternities, and women's clubs that became prominent throughout the country during the second part of the nineteenth century.[31] Between July and September of 1874, over two hundred pledges were received by societies and organizations from every part of the country to help fund the construction of the Monument. The trend underlined an important facet of the American social fabric of that era.

The social disruption brought about by industrialization and massive immigration had a major impact on the political institutions of Washington D.C. During these social changes, a great number of Protestant churches were affected by the transition. The development of the scientific vision of the world, brought forth by the

---

Guarneri, and David Alvarez, ed., Religion and Society in the American West, New York, University Press, 1987. p. 240

[31] Between 1880 and 1900, more than 460 associations were formed in the U.S.

Darwinian evolutionary theories, challenged some fundamental beliefs and tenets of the Christian faith. Fraternities like the Masonry provided its members with a network of sanctuaries for the Old Testament precepts.

The great influx of immigrants disrupted the basis of a stable social order inaugurated by the Anglo-Saxon elite, of which George Washington was promoted as a symbol. Hence, the brotherhood was a male political haven against the foreign invasion that threatened the nation at its foundation. It gave its members a sense of cohesion against the constant changes and chaos of the outside world. But mostly, the organization was a stronghold to promote true "Americanism".[32]

The order relied on a national network of loyal members, some of whom were among the most powerful men in the country. These ramifications made it an effective **hierarchy.** To protect their efficiency as a group, and to keep the higher hierarchy from public scrutiny, the new members were sworn to secrecy of its rituals. Yet the fraternity was not so much preoccupied with any esotericism inasmuch as to keep from public view a number of secret procedures, signs, and passwords used in the rituals which brought the brethren step by step one echelon closer to the "light".

The oath of secrecy also enforced among the members a sense of cohesion and fraternity which inspired unity and the idea of belonging. It also delineated and separated their sacred internal male world from the profane and chaotic world outside. The brethrens, in other words, set themselves "apart" from the uninitiated masses.

sacred	vs	*profane*
the brotherhood	vs	the outside world
order	vs	chaos and strife
secrecy	vs	darkness
temperance	vs	helplessness
men	vs	women

The ritual of initiation gave the brethren a sense of election, while the boundaries of the Masonic temple reinforced the separation between the inside and the outside world. The temple morally and physically edified a sacred asylum against the non-initiated profane world.

•

[32] See the book by Lynn Dumenil, Freemasonry and American Culture, 1880-1930, New Jersey, Princeton University Press, 1984, 70.

Among the primary targets of the brotherhood's suspicion was the Roman Catholic Church. The order apparently believed that the Church had a plan to convert the entire nation and, as a final objective, to replace the president by the Pope. They viewed the Catholic priests as diabolical, and their parishioners as sheeps devoid of any will.

This anti-Catholic sentiment was exemplified earlier by the theft of the cornerstone sent by the Pope. The consequence of these actions discloses to what extent they went to exclude from the edification of the Monument any Roman Catholic content.

The suspicion was equally shared by the Catholic Church. The mutual distrust is but a distant echo of the split brought about by the Reformation, which consequences we have discussed in the former chapter. The ensuing religious antagonism in Europe explains the scope of the animosity between Catholics and Protestants that continued to thrive in North America.

On April 20th, 1884, less than a year before the inauguration of the Monument, Pope Leo XIII issued the Encyclical *Humanum Genus,* condemning Freemasonry.[33] The Papal letter criticized the brotherhood for "rising up against God Himself" and "despoiling the nations of Christendom". The Pope further argued that the reason for the brotherhood's obsession with the secrecy of its members was devised to hide the insidious designs of its leaders so to escape any retribution. Not surprisingly, Freemasonry was increasingly seen as a danger and a challenge to the Church's authority in a politically troubled Italy. They were suspected of secretly fomenting to infiltrate all political ranks in order to promote secular ideas and finally to unseat the Church of its political powers.[34]

It is during the XIXth century that a schism between the "regular" and the "irregular" Masonry lodges appeared. The first, which were not condemned by the Church, upheld the reference of "the Great Architect of the Universe"—God. They did not get involved in

---

[33] Leo XIII, *Humanum Genus,* April 20th 1884, in, The Papal Encyclicals, 1878-1903, Raleigh, McGrath Publishing C., 1981, 91-101. He was not the only Pope to condemn the brotherhood. Others were: Benedict XIV, Pius VII, Pius VIII, Gregory XVI, Pius IX. The Catholic Church was not the only denomination in the U.S. to warn against lodge affiliation. Among them: the Lutheran Church-Missouri Synod, the Wisconsin Evangelical Lutheran Synod, the Christian Reformed Church, Church of the Brethren, Assemblies of God, Society of Friends (Quakers), Mennonites, Church of the Nazarene, Jehovah's Witnesses, The Church of Jesus Christ of Latter-day Saints (Mormons), United Brethren, Wesleyan, the Free Methodist churches, and the Seventh-day Adventist Church. General Booth of the Salvation Army also condemned the organization. Finally, in 1874, the National Christian Association coordinated a Protestant opposition to secret societies. However, the ban was not strictly enforced.

[34] These hostilities go back even farther in time; as early as 1738, Pope Clement XII had already threatened to excommunicate anyone belonging to the order.

politics, respected all faiths and churches, and were not *secretive*.[32] The second group, however, deleted the reference to "the Great Architect of the Universe", it called for the ruin of the papacy and the Church in Italy. In France, it was responsible for the anti-clerical laws of the Third Republic. It is this *secretive* type of Masonry that was condemned by the Church.

The repercussions of the sectarian antagonism can be outlined as such:

secular asceticism	vs	*collective asceticism*
the brotherhood	vs	the Catholic Church
secretive	vs	visible hierarchy
individualism	vs	collectivism
free enterprise	vs	obedience to the Church

•

The Masons' ample involvement in the funding as well as at the inauguration of the Monument provides proof of their extensive influence on American politics as a whole. The project embodied a conviction in the American way of life of which George Washington is the prototype. They made sure that the erected structure laid the foundation for a healthy "Americanism" so to endure the onslaught of any "moral degeneracy" from the chaotic world outside. The man, the Monument, the brethren, stand visibly erect at the center of the capital and point at all these ideals.

As we have seen, the distinction between the purely secular, the mythical, and the religious is blurred in the process of the edification of the Monument of George Washington. The mythical preempted and transcended any divisions between any strict religious denominations and political factions in society to become *ipso facto* a supra-religious reality. A religion above all other religions, an American civil religion.

C. Moody Plummer of the *Trestleboard* was only more extreme than most when he declared Protestantism itself to be a religion of warring sects "as intolerant often of each other as human action can be," while Masonry was "the only religion which can become universal and is [therefore] true religion."[36]

---

[35] In Great Britain, the "regular" Masonry scrupulously obeys a law requiring it to provide its membership list to Justice.

[36] Ibid. Carl Guarneri, 236.

American civil religion

The term "civil religion" comes from the work of Jean-Jacques Rousseau, THE SOCIAL CONTRACT.[37] Robert N. Bellah applied the title to the American political arena to outline the religious content of the inaugural speeches delivered by American presidents.[38]

The idea of an American civil religion first came to his attention with John F. Kennedy's inaugural address on January 20, 1961. He noticed that his address was full of religious references to God and the nation, described in very idyllic form. He also noticed that most of the past presidents' inaugural speeches had the same type of references: a call for devotion to the nation described in its ideal form, where the divine Providence plays a guiding role in shaping the destiny of the United States of America.

Four statutes of the J.F.K. inaugural speech:

a) The right to independence: "Laws of Nature and Nature's God".

b) All "are endowed by their Creator with certain inalienable Rights".

c) God is witness to America's good will: "The Supreme Judge of the world for the rectitude of our intentions".

d) the U.S. reliance on God's Providence: "a firm reliance on the protection of divine Providence".

Except for the references that allude directly to a biblical God, Bellah observes that the content of most speeches do not advocate any particular religious creed. There is no specific mention of Jesus Christ or Yahweh, for instance, since the purpose of the discourses is to form a consensus and represent the multicultural aspect of the society to which they are addressed.[29]

Yet Bellah notes that among the first presidents many also use references to the Bible. Especially to suggest a connection between the **New World** and Israel, the Exodus, the Chosen People, the promised land and the New Jerusalem.

---

[37] Jean-Jacques Rousseau, The Social Contract, in, The Essential Rousseau, New York, New American Library, 1974.

[38] Robert N. Bellah, Beyond Belief, New York, Harper & Row, 1970, 168-189.

[39] George Washington's first inaugural address of April 30, 1789 alludes to God as the "Almighty Being". It is a good example of his deist Masonic interpretation of the divinity.

These analogies, in the context of a predominantly Protestant background of the first presidents, were inevitable.

Although Bellah acknowledges the connections with Judeo-Christianism, he carefully dispels any suggestions that American civil religion has any rigid traditional Christian content or origin, or is a substitute for Christianity. He contends that civil religion has a different role and function than religion, since it is specifically political. As such, it appeals to all the people of all backgrounds. To Bellah, American civil religion is an understanding of the American experience in terms of a "transcendent ethical vision".[40] This interpretation of the universal and transcendental is only meaningful if made in relation to the origin and destiny of the U.S. political model of freedom and democracy. Bellah further points out that the God of civil religion is a God of order and freedom rather than of love and forgiveness. It is a God mostly concerned with the history and destiny of the United States.

The American civil religion attracted a great deal of attention among the intellectuals of the nineteen seventies. Despite Bellah's success there was plenty of criticism, most of which was directed at the author's definition of "religion". Especially questionable was the universal validity of its meaning. In this respect, a more appropriate term to describe it is Paul Tillich's definition of "quasi-religion".[41]

Most of the Founding Fathers had a Christian background, more specifically, Protestant, since most of them emigrated from Europe. With this in mind, the American civil definition of religion is limited by these cultural and geographical parameters. This view of religion, for instance, ignores the aboriginal cultures that were present at the time of the foundation of this nation. It makes the natives conspicuously "invisible".[42] Furthermore, there is no mention of the cultures brought by the Americans of African descent.[43]

The combat against ferocious beasts; the wars of "the Israelites

---

[40] Robert N. Bellah, The Broken Covenant, New York, A Crossroad Book, 1975, 142.

[41] Paul Tillich distinguishes "pseudo" from "quasi-religion". The first is an intended and deceptive similarity with religion, whereas the second indicates a genuine similarity which is not necessarily intended. See, Christianity and the Encounter of the World Religions, New York, Columbia University Press, 1963, 5f.

[42] Charles H. Long, Civil Rights, Civil Religion: Visible People and Invisible People, in, AMERICAN CIVIL RELIGION, ed. by Russel E. Richey and Donald G. Jones, New York, Harper Forum Books, 1974.

[43] Appropriately labeled by Ralph Ellison as the "Invisible Man". Ralph Ellison, Invisible Man, New York, Vintage Books, 1972.

against the Philistines," of "God's chosen people against the Indian Gentiles."[44]

The religious persecution from which the first settlers escaped in Europe is reinstated against the cultures of the natives and the slaves in America. The antagonistic patterns of the Old World are restored in the New. The sacred reality of the newly instituted United States of America is based on the cultural and religious exclusion of the profane reality of the heathens and the pagans, of which the Zuni Pueblo is one typical example.

sacred	vs	*profane*
God of order	vs	natives and slaves
Judeo-Christianity	vs	heathens and pagans
United States	vs	aboriginal & African cultures

American civil religion, as outlined by Bellah, is a supra-political institution predominantly concerned with Judeo-Christian precepts. The historical foundations and later developments edified and maintained the image of George Washington as the prototype of the American civil religion. This ethical model and the hierarchy of political power was set at the beginning. The "American" New Order originated by the Founding Fathers was appropriately sustained to preserve their sacred "power", as illustrated by the number of presidents since Washington who have been Anglo-Saxon, Protestant, and white. Because of this pattern set by the Fathers in the beginning, the Anglo-Saxons believe they have a divine and mythical birthright to be **elected** president. That premise was consecrated at the outset by the inauguration of the George Washington National Monument, the primal model of the presidency. The only exception is John Kennedy, a Catholic, who was killed in office.

To that effect, the Roman saying captures the essence of sovereignty and rule of politics, *cujus regio, ejus religio:* the religion of the rulers becomes the political creed of the land.

As we have seen, myth plays a considerable part in the evolution and integration of ideology. The power behind the language of myth is to define, confine, and control the scope of the national identity. By the same token, it shapes a meaningful consensus in the whole collectivity.

---

[44] By Isaac M. Wise in a lecture given at the Theological Library Association of Cincinnati, January 7, 1868. From, Conrad Cherry ed, God's New Israel, New Jersey, Prentice Hall, 1971, 224.

American civil religion, as it relies on its governmental institutions and on the presidency—in terms of the charisma of the office —embodies and fulfills in many respects the same function as religion. As Bellah observed: "The answer is that the separation of church and state has not denied the political realm of a religious dimension."[45] This remark introduces yet another very complex point of contention: the separation of church and state. Bellah brings up the question briefly but does not clarify the issue. No doubt there is a danger, more so today because of the effective use of mass-media in the creation of a national consensus. But also because the religious and the political may be identified or confused as a single and legitimate reality by a greater number of people living in a secularized world. As a consequence, the State becomes the only unquestionable source of economical power and political "truth". This theological "truth" is amply suggested by the symbol that epitomizes the relation between Freemasonry, politics, the economy, and civil religion in America.

$1 IN GOD WE TRUST $1

On one side of the dollar bill we have the portrait of our celebrated hero. On the other side, a symbol of Freemasonry: the pyramid crowned by the all-seeing-eye inside the pyramidion. The latter also represents the zenith of political power overseeing the pyramidal order of hierarchy. And at the center of the bill is the caption that embraces the creed in the power of money, that ultimate icon of American civil religion.

There is an even greater paradox inherent in the inaugurating process of the presidency. The ritual of swearing-in. It was initiated by George Washington himself on April 30, 1789, when he added "so help me God", and kissed the Bible. All presidents since have abided to the ritual.

With one hand on the Bible, all presidents have stood in front of the judge and have sworn of their true intentions. The whole nation and God as their witness. The presidential oath, however, presents an evangelical contradiction. The New Testament, on which one of the presidential hands lays, is explicit:

---

[45] Robert N. Bellah, Beyond Belief, New York, Harper & Row, 1970, 171.

Mt. 5:33 Again you have heard that it was said to the men of old, 'You shall not swear falsely, but shall perform to the Lord what you have sworn.' But I say to you, Do not swear at all, either by heaven, for it is the throne of God, or by the earth, for it is his footstool, or by Jerusalem, for it is the city of the great King. And do not swear by your head, for you cannot make one hair white or black. Let what you say be simply 'Yes' or 'No'; anything more than this comes from evil.[46]

---

[46] The word "evil" is also translated into "the evil one".

An Outlook on the World of Mythology

In the midst of the street of the city, and on either side of the river, was the tree of life with its twelve kinds of fruit, yielding its fruit each month; and the leaves of the tree were for the healing of the nations.

Revelation, 22:2

In the image making of George Washington that we have just outlined, the idyllic side of the hero was emphasized and the timeless aspect of his being was promoted, creating in the process an icon of mythical proportions. In retrospect, the mythologizing crusade of the nineteenth century became the cornerstone of a true "Americanism".[1] As a result, the Founding Father was consecrated as a prototype of the American *mythos* as well as its *ethos.* Both are enshrined in the monument that points to the heavens. This myth-making consecration shows how important and significant a role the mythical process plays in the creation of a collective identity.

Other mythical processes have been efficient in ideology. Marxism is a point in case. It is well known that Marxist ideology is based on the **antagonism** between the classes, promoting the quest for a classless society as its ends.

---

[1] As Claude Lévi-Strauss pointed out: "I am not far from believing that, in our own societies, history has replaced mythology and fulfills the same function, that for societies without writing and without archives the aim of mythology is to ensure that as closely as possible —complete closeness is obviously impossible—the future will remain faithful to the present and to the past . . . But nevertheless the gap which exists in our mind to some extent between mythology and history can probably be breached by studying histories which are conceived as not at all separated from but as a continuation of mythology."; in, Myth and Meaning, Toronto, University of Toronto Press, 1978, 42-43.

classless society

the bourgeois class   vs   the working class

Marxists have used a compelling propaganda tool. As history reveals, the political application of the mythical supplants one adversary by another. The bourgeoisie is replaced by the dictatorship of the proletariat. The end result is that one oppressive hierarchy is simply substituted by another. Consequently, the world of politics never escapes the dilemma of eternal opposition between its polarities. It never attains the purely transcendental character of the wholly other.

Ideology merely uses myth's seductive powers to propagate its own political ends. Nazism, Fascism, and to a certain extent some forms of nationalism and patriotism, typify the seductive powers decreed in national myths. The propagation of these myths take hold of the "masses". They end up subverting the rights of the individual and drag the "people" into nationalistic or patriotic frenzies.

It remains that the real essence of the religious does not stem from an idealized past or regressive antagonisms. Such sterile aversions are detrimental to our world. The nuclear arms race that resulted from the blind opposition between the U.S. and the U.S.S.R. can now destroy our world many times over. This type of antagonism only served to bolster radical communist and capitalist ideologies on both sides. In the meantime, Japan and Germany were free to challenge the U.S.' economic power.

The truly religious is only possible through the **whole** dynamic interactive process of the sacred and the profane into the wholly other, where the whole religious and cultural reality is acknowledged and transcended. Only with love and openness is this experience possible.

True spiritualism should also promote a healthy dynamic between the self and the collectivity. It should divert any attempt by the collectivity to subvert the rights of the individual. And by the same token it should denigrate any individual greed and selfishness that exploits and destroys the social fabric. As Martin Luther King suggested:

> Perhaps I must turn my faith to the inner spiritual church, the church within the church, as the true *ekklesia* and the hope of the world.[2]

---

[2] Martin Luther King, Jr, "Letter from Birmingham Jail", April 16, 1963, from, Why We Can't Wait, New York, Harper & Row, Publishers, Martin Luther King Jr. Copyright 1963.

214

As we look around our world, the mythologization seems to have overwhelmed the cultural and political process. Especially since a greater number of people have become secularized by the prevailing power of the mass-media. TV may have become the new opium of the people. The extent to which America is ruled by such a powerful medium should be studied carefully. The survival of freedom depends on it.

It is important to stress at this point that at the core of the great National Monument are the ultimate principles of "life, liberty, and the pursuit of happiness". The hero's cultural, political, religious, or sectarian traits are secondary. And more important, they should not be confused. The principles of life and the pursuit of freedom supplant any other prerogative. They are the underlying bond of the United States of America. And no cultural or ethnical precedence should hinder its pursuit. As Joseph Campbell puts it:

> For any god who is not transparent to transcendence is an idol, and its worship is idolatry.[3]

Political unity is a fundamental element in the progress of the **United States.** It is unfortunate, however, that "multiculturalism" is seen by its detractors as a threat to national identity. It should not be so, since the foundation of nationality is based on the **Spirit** of the Constitution and the Bill of Rights. Isn't the European Community made up of a multitude of cultures and languages? Actually, the emergence of the multi-cultural affirmation in the U.S. is but a confirmation of the principle of freedom. True unity ultimately lies in the **quest** for freedom for all, regardless of race or creed. Perhaps the greatest form of tribalism is not the affirmation of cultural diversity but the imposition of an atavistic "Americanism".

•

Today, the mythical process is active everywhere. Some of these mythical functions are reflected in sports. **Fan**atics gather in bowl shaped stadiums which, if seen from up high, have the appearance of lively mandalas. Some fans will openly admit that going to a ball game is like going to church. The purely religious is slowly being replaced by America's other cultic pastime: the sport event. Football and baseball have been openly labeled as a "religion". The stadium has replaced the temple as the place for collective gathering and mysticism. At the singing of the national anthem, for instance,

---

[3] Joseph Campbell, The Inner Reaches of Outer Space, Harper & Row, San Francisco, Publishers, 1988, 44.

people stand up with hands on their hearts, eyes staring at the sky, chanting the sacred hymn in honor of the state.

Fans and foes alike congregate to witness a primal **antagonism** between rival teams in what is a grand exhibit of "morality play":[4]

local team	vs	outsiders
fans	vs	foes
the winners	vs	the losers

At stake is the **struggle** for victory. Everything evolves around the pursuit of a single and elusive object: the ball. The final outcome is the quest for a national—the super-bowl—or even international—the world cup—recognition.

The mythical aspect of these events goes back to the very origin of the Olympic games themselves. They began in ancient Greece (776 BC) in honor of Zeus, the supreme god of Greek mythology. The games eventually reappeared in the late nineteenth century as a symbol of international **competition.**

There is yet another important aspect of American mythology: Hollywood, the movie-land "center" of the world. The projected gods and goddesses on the silver screen are but creations of ethereal beings from an-**other** world.

Superman, Batman, Wonder Woman, Dick Tracy, Bugs Bunny, Mickey Mouse, etc., all have become part of the American *mythos*. Each outlines one or the other aspect of the cultural *psyche*. Think of the idolization of Marilyn Monroe. The celebrity cult has gone as far as worshipping and even resurrecting certain stars. Elvis, for instance, was seen alive again.

Like myth, the stars of cinema and TV are beings that are separated from ordinary life by the **story**. The heroes are fictitious beings that live in a separate movie-land. Communication with these beings is impossible. Their "world" is inaccessible to the spectator. The characters brought to life through the medium are set "apart" from the viewer. They evolve in a universe separate from the profane reality of our world. Their stories present a self-enclosed world distinct from ours. In movies everything is possible, the heroes live according to a different set of rules. The mass-media as a result has become the new vehicle for the mystery of the supernatural. A prerogative formerly held by religion.

---

[4] See the article in the Wall Street Journal, by William M. Bulkeley, entitled: As Johnny Most Tells It, Basketball Pits Good vs. Evil, April 21, 1989.

216

Hollywood has not only become the image-making center of the American *mythos,* but of its *ethos* as well.

What has been said above about the mythologizing function of mass-media should not come as a surprise to most. But it might come as a surprise to some if we say that science is heavily involved in the mythologizing process of our western culture.

Nothing bears more mythological analogy than theories about the **big bang.** The physicists' preoccupation with the origin of the world is nothing new to mythology. Most if not all mythologies have theories about the beginning of the world. And all the myths are believed to be true stories by the people who live by them. Mircea Eliade coined this passion for the beginning, *regressus ad uterum:* a longing for the origin.[5]

•

Throughout our analysis, antagonism plays an essential part in the edification of identity. The opposition between the French and English cultures in Canada have polarized both sides. The struggle has hardened the positions, radicalized the views.

The quest for independence and the desire to be "distinct" elevated the ideal of being **separate** from the rest of Canada. The quest embodies a yearning to be set "apart" from those who are perceived as the "other". It amplifies the opposition between the "us" and "them".

Even Robert Bourassa, Quebec's prime minister, admits that the idea of being a "distinct society" is to a certain extent "symbolic".[6] This would explain how the Old Testament typology of being "chosen" plays such a great part in religion.

Yet the essence of true religious experience does not lie in the "tribal" and ethnocentric belief of being "distinct" or "chosen".[7] Although cultural and religious roots are essential and are an integral part of the religious development, the true spiritual experience lies in the openness to the **other:** moving from the exclusive to the all inclusive wholly other.

---

[5] If there is an object of idolatry in our modern cultures it is the car. The automobile may also have become a symbolic metal womb. As it moves the occupant, it also isolates and shields the driver from the outside world. It wraps and bundles his whole existence. It allows the driver to experience a *regressus ad uterum,* a return to maternal roots. Perhaps the loud pounding music of the "boom machines" reminds the young driver of the thumping sound of the mother's heartbeat while he was a fetus.

[6] "**Q: Why did you need the "distinct society" clause in the constitution? A . . .** It was symbolic to some extent. We were not saying we need additional powers." In, Time Magazine, July 9, 1990, vol. 136, No. 2.

[7] "But nationalism, perhaps better called tribalism, is an enduring phenomenon, and one that looks more enduring than the map of the world as it is drawn in the late twentieth century." From, "Goodbye to the Nation State?"; in, The Economist, June 23, 1990, Vol. 315, No. 7660.

As we have seen in Exodus, Moses did not set foot in the promised land. What the story reveals is that the **quest** is at the origin of true religious experience, not possession of the land. It is during the journey in the desert that Yahweh gave him the ten commandments. Inaugurating in the process a bond between God, the Prophet, and Israel.

•

The mythical quest in Quebec has kept the political debate in Canada animated.

The deadline of June 23, 1990, to ratify the Meech Lake constitutional accord to help mend a divided Canada was disregarded. Unanimity between the participants could not be reached. As a result, Canada has been left at a political crossroad.

As hope for the accord subsided, the ultimate question remained: will Quebec take another step to further consolidate an exclusive identity for itself and leave behind the mold of "opposition" which has been the source of its national identity? Or will Quebec transcend its nationalistic concerns and redirect its efforts toward a new type of political union with the rest of the provinces? History reveals that the dynamic relationship between Quebec and Canada has been the source of Quebec's national identity. The dynamic between the cultural entities also made Canada a model country respected throughout the world for its democratic system, health care, social justice, and economic development.

The death of the accord stemmed primarily from the rejection by certain factions of the "distinct society" clause specifically included to bring Quebec back into constitutional talks. On June 23rd, Premier Clyde Wells of Newfoundland, who was against the special status for Quebec, ignored the deadline and adjourned the house assembly without a vote to ratify the accord, killing the last hope for an accord in the process.

The other major opponent was Manitoba's New Democratic Party elected member Elijah Harper, a native Ojibway Cree. During the crux constitutional debate, Harper, the only "Indian" of the elected assembly, used all his energy to block the passage of the accord in the provincial legislature. He succeeded. As a result, he became a symbol for centuries of aboriginal resentment toward the power of the white establishment. Harper's resolve prompted the leader of the Assembly of Manitoba Chiefs Phil Fontaine to declare:

Harper represents the collective will of the Indian peoples of Manitoba and Canada, and their pain and disappointment over

218

the dishonorable treatment they have received from this nation.[8]

The North America natives have finally found a way to be heard.

Native indignation started as soon as the constitutional debate touched on Quebec's demand to be recognized as a "distinct society", making the francophones of Quebec and the anglophones of the rest of the country the two founding cultures of Canada, and in the process ignoring the natives as the primal cultures of their own homeland.

Their resentment of constitutional matters is nothing new. In 1867, the British North American Act, which constituted Canada as a country, mentions the natives in a nominal way, stating only that the lands reserved for them fell under the authority of the Canadian Parliament. The happy event that saw the birth of Canada was for the aboriginal peoples the beginning of their misgivings. The new government of Canada began its political life by ignoring "Indian" claims for self rule. Denying them the right to promote their own culture.

A few years later, in 1876, the adoption of the Indian Act finally granted the aboriginal people the status of "Indians". The Act entitled the natives to free education and eventually exempted them from paying taxes. Although the Act was meant as a privilege, it soon became apparent that it further alienated the natives from being regarded as fully fledged citizens with the power to control their own lands and destinies. The extent to which the natives were belittled by the Act is revealed by its content which promised the "Indians" that if they acted in a "civilized" manner and moved out of the reserves they would be allowed to apply for full citizenship.

The full right to vote in a federal election was only granted to all natives in 1960.

Ignoring the primal character of the native cultures is perhaps the biggest obstacle in the constitutional debate in Canada. Only with the recognition of the **profane** reality embodied by the natives could new hope arise. Only then could a new vision of the country be generated.

The native cultural reality is exemplified in this book by the Zuni Pueblo. We have seen how close to nature they are. Something lacking in our western civilization. In addition, their culture does not reflect the misconceptions we might have had about them. Or

---

[8] Maclean's; Canada's Weekly Newsmagazine, July 2, 1990, 28.

the misguided way in which they have been portrayed by Hollywood. Old movies single them out as the savage heathen, the enemy of liberty. They were blamed for being a major obstacle to the colonization and evangelization of the New World. As history shows, the sacred belief in the superiority of the Christian faith was enough to justify the taking of their land, rejecting their religious and cultural traditions as paganism in the process. Hollywood, however, may have finally taken up the lost cause of the natives in movies like *Dances with Wolves.*

•

We have talked about the "sociocentric" approach to religion that infers that it is foremost a social dynamic generated by collectivity.[9] According to this theory, society and its structures supersede the individual and even supplant him. On the opposite side of the spectrum, theology, which is defined as the interpretation of the Word of God, relies strictly on the "Word" as the only source of religious truth. For Christian theologians the authority of the "Word" of the Bible could not be questioned. Yet both play an important role in the dynamic interrelation between religion and the religious. The first is integrated by the social systems of beliefs and practices, the second is regenerated by the individual, typified here by Christ.

Christ challenged the powers of this world. As an **individual** he questioned the institutions and the laws that stood for them, showing that the real essence of the religious lies in the dynamic interaction between the individual and society as a **whole.** Jesus the man, and Christ the God, come together as a dynamic interaction between the individual and the assembly, where it fulfills the Christian goal of history.

Yet Jesus Christ is best described as the individual embodiment of the sacred tradition of the **Scriptures** and the sum product of the historical contradictions of the society in which he lived and died. Christ transcended the strict sacred beliefs imposed by Judaism and the priests of his time.

Nonetheless, the established religion in Jesus' times perceived his message as a threat to the social structure. As a result, they crucified him. This whole process set forth the regeneration of old re-

---

[9] Sociological interpretation of religion has been for more than a century a popular method of interpreting religious phenomena. In the late nineteen seventies, a new branch of religious studies was created at the University of Quebec in Montreal (UQAM). It is called "religiology". This new approach proposes that the study of religion should be interpreted from a strictly scientific perspective. There are two predominant approaches to religiology: the sociological and the phenomenological study of the religious phenomena.

ligious precepts into new Christian beliefs. Furthermore, his death was not an obstacle to his message but rather the **beginning** of his other-worldly reality which turned out to be Christianity.

The more one studies the period in which Jesus made his appearance, the more one finds that everything converged toward the event of Jesus Christ as a spiritual messiah, rather than a messianic revolutionary, who would favor the new Christian faith to spread throughout the Roman empire.

After a lengthy period of independence under the Hasmonaeans, the Jews did not view kindly the presence of the Romans in Judaea. Even though the priests were in control of the Jerusalem temple, the antagonistic fervor of the Zealots inflamed the political situation. The nationalists were impatiently awaiting a sign from God that would signal Rome's impending fall. Messianic hopes were high among the resurgents who wanted to restore Israel to its glorious past. A national revolt against Rome was gaining momentum.

Menahem, the son of the Zealot leader Judas the Galilaean, first seized control of Massada and afterward marched to Jerusalem and eventually gained control of the city (66 AD). In Jerusalem, Menahem was killed by one of the followers of the priest Eleazar. He was murdered in retaliation for Eleazar's father who died at the hands of the Zealots during the invasion of Jerusalem. The rivalries among Jewish factions soon faded as they shared a common hatred for the Romans. As a result, Joseph ben Gorion with the help of the high priest took charge of the city's defense.

The news of Nero's suicide, and the ensuing civil war in Rome, was perceived as the sign that the empire was on the brink of collapse. Hopes that the kingdom of Israel could be restored were high.

Ps. 72:8 May we have dominion from sea to sea, and from the River to the ends of the earth!

Rome did not fall. Vespasian and his troops, who were already in control of the greater part of Palestine, were waiting for the appropriate time to invade Jerusalem. Before he could attack he was recalled to Rome where his partisans had seized power on his behalf. Before his departure, he left the command of his troops to his eldest son. In April of 70 AD, Titus invaded Jerusalem. Nationalist resistance was fierce but the Romans prevailed. On August 29, the same day the First Temple was destroyed by the Babylonians in 587 BC, the sanctuary of the second temple was set on fire.

As Jerusalem lay in ruins, the Jews who survived were enslaved and brought to Rome to be scattered throughout the Roman empire.

221

As the revolutionary hopes were crushed, a movement of spiritual salvation emerged.

The Spirit that filled the Christians would eventually spread throughout the limits of the empire and beyond.

•

During his life on earth Jesus worked wonders on the people he touched. As he left this world, he gave his followers the enormous responsibility to go and make disciples from **all** the nations baptizing them in the name of the Father, the Son, and the **Holy Spirit.**

As we have seen, among the three persons the Holy Spirit is the most mysterious. It is a ghostly personification which suggests a disembodied being of a genderless nature. We have also shown how the Holy Spirit personifies the profane nature of God. How the hidden, the excluded, the overshadowed, becomes an interactive and dynamic reality with the holy in God. And how the overshadowed reality of the Mother of God at the conception of Christ is a privileged **sign** of the hidden nature of the Holy Ghost.

The Holy Spirit deliberately comes over Mary to veil the profane character of her being. Similarly, the Holy Ghost becomes a metaphor for the shrouded and obscure nature of the profane in all religious experiences. Yet Mary's womb becomes not only the symbol of Christ's birth but the "door" to the true meaning of life in the world.

In ancient Judaism, and in Jesus' times, women could not approach the holy, they were excluded from its vicinity. They were literally the property of men, their subordinates. Deuteronomy is specific. The adulterous man is violating the husband's or father's property rights not the woman's.[10] Women were regarded as nonentities. They were only valued for their childbearing capabilities— and that too fell under man's control. As such, the progeny and lineage, which was man's prized possession, became the supervision of patriarchal religious practices.

These examples and many more give some insight as to why the goddess Asherah and her female counterparts were deliberately eradicated from the theological discourses of the Pentateuch. Continuous efforts were made by the Israelite religious hierarchy to keep the population away from the popular Goddess worship that was prevalent in ancient Near-East at the times of the compilation of the Bible. It explains the prophets' relentless **struggle** against the "harlotry" of the Canaanite religion of which Asherah was perhaps the most popular deity. Her fertility cults challenged the foundation

---

[10] Deut. 22:28-29.

of monotheism as well as the theological justification for partriarchal dominion over women.

> Gen. 3:14 The LORD God said to the serpent,
> "Because you have done this,
> cursed are you above all cattle,
> and above all wild animals;
> upon your belly you shall go,
> and dust you shall eat
> all the days of your life
> I will put enmity between you and
> the woman . . .
> To the woman he said,
> "I will greatly multiply your pain in
> childbearing;
> in pain you shall bring forth
> children,
> yet your desire shall be for your
> husband,
> and he shall rule over you."

•

Among the innumerable names found in the Old Testament, the one that represents the core of Jewish identity is **Israel.** As we have seen already, the etymology of the name is revealing. It implies the **strife** and **struggle** of "man" with God or its angels. As such, it is one of the more enlightening principles of the religious experience. We have described at length how the **opposition** is an essential feature in the edification of identity in general and of the sacred in particular. Antagonism allows the possibility of openness. However, it is important to stress as we conclude, that it is not the **dichotomy** *per se* that is central but the dynamic interaction itself. All of the examples of **duality** in this book are used as a heuristic tool to help understand the process of the sacred edification and identification. The identity of the sacred or profane is merely relative. It is the **dynamic** itself that sets the identities apart. They can take any shape or form depending on the hierophany. Furthermore, the identity of the sacred is important only as a stage in the development of true spiritual experience. It becomes truly religious when it interacts with the profane into the "fuzzy" field of the wholly other.

Similarly, the sacred quality of being distinct, or to be set "apart", is only an **exclusive** part of the wholly other experience, which by definition includes the profane in the all **inclusive** whole.

When the holy reverts itself into the **exclusive,** as it happens in fanaticism displayed in all religions, it excludes the realm of the universal, the truly religious. It is the dynamic opposition between the sacred and the profane that enhances the possibilities of openness toward the wholly other. It is the interaction between the center, the exclusively other, and the periphery, in other words, the inclusively other, that opens the way to the wholly other.

Yet only with the recognition of the profane reality, typified here by the Goddess as an integral part of the religious dynamic, could the spiritual experience be complete. Only when we "surrender" to the whole dynamic process of the **wholly other** can we experience the religious.

God of the Fathers dominated Judaism, and God the Son, Christianity. Perhaps a true "partnership" with God the Mother is in our future.[11]

---

[11] See Riane Eisler and David Loye's, The Partnership Way, San Francisco, Harper & Row, 1991.

ACKNOWLEDGEMENTS

Permission to quote excerpts from the following sources is gratefully acknowledged.

Blake, William, "The Marriage of Heaven and Hell", from, "The Complete Writings of William Blake", Oxford, Oxford University Press, 1969. Reprinted by permission of Oxford University Press.

Bellah, Robert N., "Beyond Belief", New York, Harper & Row Publishers Inc., 1970. Copyright ©1984 by the Robert Bellah Trust. Reprinted by permission.

Campbell, Joseph, "The Inner Reaches of Outer Space", San Francisco, Harper & Row Publishers Inc., 1986. Copyright ©1986 by Harper & Row Publishers Inc. 1986. Reprinted by permission.

Cherry, Conrad, ed. by, "God's New Israel", New York, Prentice Hall, 1971. Copyright ©1971 by Prentice Hall Inc. Reprinted by permission.

Cunliffe, Marcus, "George Washington; Man and Monument", Boston, Little, Brown & Company Inc., 1958. Copyright ©1958 by Marcus Cunliffe. Reprinted by permission.

Davies, Robertson, "What's Bred in the Bone", Toronto, Penguin Books Canada Ltd., 1985. Copyright ©1985 by Robertson Davies. Reprinted by permission.

Durkheim, Emile & Mauss, Marcel, "Primitive Classification", Chicago, University of Chicago Press, 1963. Copyright ©1963 University of Chicago Press. Reprinted by permission.

The Economist, from the article entitled, "Goodbye to the Nation State?", June 23, 1990. Copyright ©1990 by The Economist Newspaper Limited. Reprinted by permission.

France, Anatole, "Le Crime de Sylvestre Bonnard", Paris, les Editions Gallimard. Out of copyright and in the public domain.

Girard, René, "The Scapegoat", Baltimore, Johns Hopkins University Press, 1986. Copyright ©1986 by The Johns Hopkins University Press. Reprinted by permission.

Green, Jesse, ed. by, "Zuni, Selected Writings by Frank Hamilton Cushing", Lincoln, University of Nebraska Press, 1979. Copyright ©1979, by University of Nebraska Press. Reprinted by permission.

Guarneri, Carl & Alvarez, David, ed. by, "Religion and Society in the American West", Lanham, University Press of America Inc., 1979. Copyright ©1979 by University Press of America Inc. (R). Reprinted by permission.

King, Martin Luther Jr., "Letter from Birmingham Jail" April 16, 1963, from "Why We Can't Wait", New York, Harper Collins Publishers, 1963. Copyright ©1963 by Martin Luther King Jr. Reprinted by permission.

Lévi-Strauss, Claude, "Structural Anthropology", New York, Basic Books Inc. Publishers, 1963. Copyright ©1976 by Claude Lévi-Strauss. Reprinted by permission.

Lévi-Strauss, Claude, "Myth And Meaning", Toronto, University of Toronto Press, 1978. Copyright ©1978 by University of Toronto Press. Reprinted by permission.

Maclean's: Canada's Weekly Newsmagazine, "Drumbeats of Anger", by Brian Bergman, July 2 1990. Phil Fontaine, the Assembly of Manitoba Chiefs.

Rad von, Gerhard, "Genesis", London, SCM Press Ltd., 1969, Copyright ©1969 by Chr. Kaiser Verlag GmbH. Reprinted by permission.

Wallace, Howard N., "The Eden Narrative", Decatur, Scholars Press, 1985. Copyright ©1985 by The President and Fellows of Harvard College. Reprinted by permission.

Wilson, Ian, "Exodus the True Story", San Francisco, Harper & Row, 1985. Copyright ©1985 by Harper & Row Publishers Inc. Reprinted by permission.

Whitman, Walt, "The Complete Poetry & Collected Prose, by Walt Whitman", New York, Penguin USA. Out of copyright and in the public domain.

INDEX

ORDER FORM

Please send the following book. I understand that I may return it for a full refund, for any reason, no question asked.

GOD, MYTH, AND METAPHOR:
The Profane Reality of the Goddess

Company name: _____

Name: _____

Address: _____

City: _____ State: _____ Zip: _____

Number of copies: _____ × $14.95 = _____

Inquire about our bulk rate at the address below.

Sales Tax:

Please add 8.25% for books shipped to California addresses.

Shipping:

Book rate: $2.00 for the first book and 75 cents for each additional book (surface shipping may take three to four weeks).

Air mail: $4.50 per book.

Postal Orders:

Please send your check to:　**Northshore Publishing**
P.O. Box 25398
Los Angeles, CA 90025